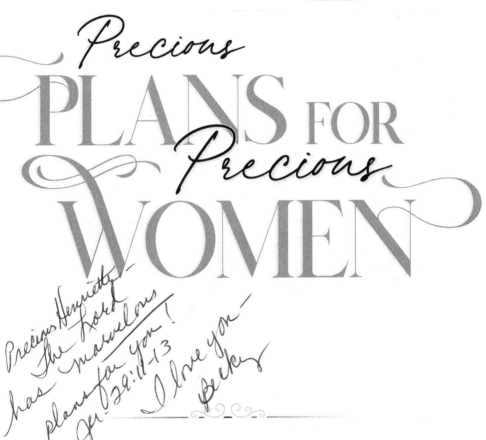

Precious PLANS FOR *Precious* WOMEN

Precious Henrietta—
The Lord
has "marvelous"
plans for you!
Jer. 29:11-13 I love you—
Becky

BECKY BLACKMON
and her mother, *Lea Fowler*

Publishing Designs, Inc.

Huntsville, Alabama

Publishing Designs, Inc.
P.O. Box 3241
Huntsville, Alabama 35810

Cover and page design: CrosslinCreative.net

Editors: Peggy Coulter and Debra G. Wright

Printed in the United States of America

Publisher's Cataloging-in-Publication Data

Blackmon, Becky 1948—
Precious Plans for Precious Women / Becky Blackmon
258 pp.
11. chapters and study questions
1. Spiritual Priorities—Women. 2. Roles in Home and Church 3. Titus 2.
I. Title.
ISBN 978-1-945127-23-6
248.8

Dedication

To the Holy Planner and Architect of our lives
and
To you, Mom. Meet you at the gate.

Special Thanks:

Trent! It's because of you I can even turn on my computer! You get it; I don't. I thank God for you. I wish I could adopt you and your entire family. By the way, your life defines the word *deacon!*

My precious, precious family, you fill my heart and life with so much love. I adore hearing you call my name—MiMi.

My praying soul sisters, what would I do without your encouragement and love? I don't ever want to know.

To my mentors: Liz, Fran, Elsie, Frances, Betty, and Tressie.

Cathy, you are my special loving friend who shares her paradise and lets me put my burdens down. You are a "Precious Woman" with so many talents, so much love, and a servant's heart. There are no words to describe how indebted I am to you. Phil is so proud of you. And I am so thankful that you are my sister. I love you.

And always to my Jeff—the one who stole my heart so long ago.

Endorsements

Becky Blackmon speaks frankly to women, unwrapping *God's Precious Plans for Precious Women* from Titus 2:3-5. Since many are not mentored by godly moms, she shares memories and teachings from her mother, Lea Fowler—and the two sing a duet of valuable life-lessons. Their insights encourage readers to seek God's guidance and pray for His plan to work in their lives.

> —Cynthia Guy, author, *The Girl for My Son*, *Sweet Truths*, *What About the Women*, and *Struggle, Seek Grow*

Becky Blackmon writes from a heart that is overflowing with love for God, His Word, and His people. In *Precious Plans for Precious Women*, she offers to Christian women everywhere a reminder of God's "Precious Plans." Becky calls women of God to a higher place. Every child of God who reads this volume will be encouraged mightily and richly blessed.

> —Jeff A. Jenkins, The Jenkins Institute

Contents

MY PLANS FOR YOU

I knew you when you first loved Me
And sought to do My will.
Your hand took Mine as we traveled
Together up the hill.

The climb has not always been pleasant;
There've been storms and thunder and rain
And times when you thought the trip futile
Because of the trials and pain.

But the longer we trudged up the mountain
And occasionally caught sight of the view,
The more you ceased to wonder
At the plans I still have for you.

—Lea Fowler

Introduction

Due to pressures of women's rights, we often conform to the teachings of the day, not realizing the final outcome of our choices. God has great plans for His daughters. How it must hurt Him to see us cut off our blessings because of lack of knowledge or lack of love for Him.

> "For I know the plans that I have for You," declares the Lord, "plans for welfare and not for calamity to give You a future and a hope. Then You will call upon Me and come and pray to Me, and I will listen to you. You will seek Me and find Me, when you search for Me with all your heart. I will be found by you," declares the Lord (Jer. 29:11–14).

May our Father help us to understand that He will bless us "far more abundantly beyond all that we ask or think according to the power that works within us" (Eph. 3:20).

It's not easy being a woman. It never has been. This book is for women and our relationships. Whether it is mother and daughter, sister to sister, or a Christian woman helping another Christian woman, we need to seek the word of God and see what our Father says about our roles.

MOM SAYS

Some ladies won't hear, and you can't "learn" anybody. Some will never want to learn. They would rather do it their way and suffer. So be it. But for those who want to learn and better themselves and be spared bitter reaping and be happier in the learning, then come and let us study together and reason together about a better way. I've heard young Christian women say, "I don't want the older women teaching me." And I have heard older women say, "I don't want to teach the younger women. I've done my time." However, I haven't heard God say, "How would you ladies like for it to be done?"

CHAPTER 1

A Woman to HELP

I thank God that He made me a woman. Like the song lyrics croon from an old musical, "I Enjoy Being a Girl!" I call myself a "girlie tomboy" because when I was younger, I loved to play ball and get dirty, but I also adored dressing up, doing hair, and applying makeup.

I have never wanted to be a man. Well, I take that back. There were occasions earlier in life when I fervently desired to be a man so I could help the church in leadership. I now know better. God has seen fit to give those positions to men, not women, and I am so thankful for that! I learned to say to myself, "No, Becky. God has made you a woman. The Father has a plan for you. He needs for you to be a woman so you can help the sisters." And the woman who showed me how to love God and help the sisters was my mom.

The Best Lap

I was raised on her lap. I was the third and last child, and Mom had little time to hold me and play with me because she was a busy mom, heavily involved with church, two older children, and a husband. So when we gathered to worship the Lord, I climbed up on her lap, took my place and reigned supreme—for at least forty-five minutes! Mom even called these moments "our time." A time for worship came to be synonymous with a time for love.

Perhaps you understand this. Maybe you are even nodding your head as you are reading. You too can recall the precious instances of childhood when you bonded with your mom, swaddled in love, and comforted on her lap. Or perhaps you remember these moments with your own daughter. It's a woman thing.

Mothers and daughters—what a powerful bond is possible. It begins in the womb and ends at the tomb. Even when one passes away and the other is left to carry on alone, the bond is still there. It never departs. The connection runs from heart to heart, and God Himself put it there.

Here is a marvelous personal story from author Mary Farrar about her relationship with her mother:

> We often talked for hours, debating and discussing the issues of life. She was always honest, open, and willing to listen at the drop of a hat. She mentored me by listening as often to my heart as to my words. I never went through a struggle that Mom did not sense it and offer wise input and encouragement. Most importantly, Mom mentored me by living in the Scriptures herself . . . When life was unclear, Mom always seemed to know where to go in Scripture to meet and address my needs. She had a firm grip of the teachings of Scripture when I most needed to hear them.[1]

She's Just Like You

As the years passed, Mom became my confidant, my teacher, my disciplinarian, and my best friend. Now don't get me wrong. She was always my mother, the woman in charge of raising me. She took raising her children as a serious job. But to me she was just Mama—the one who I could talk to, relate to, complain to—the only one who understood me. Later in life, she often told me the story of being at her wits' end with a very young, energetic, and headstrong Becky. She was frazzled and helpless, finally pouring her heart out to her best friend Nita. Nita calmly looked at her and said, "Why, Lea, she's just like you!" I think Mom figured me out that day.

There was not one single subject that I could not discuss with her—not one. Be it personal, controversial, or even taboo, she had told me, "Becky, you can ask me anything." And I did! When my children were teenagers, Mom advised me never to act shocked when they brought up questions about something lurid or objectionable. She said, "Just act normal, nod your head, and reply, 'Oh, that's interesting. Let me think about that a minute.'" She always reassured me that I could pass out later.

We delighted in one another's company. Yes, we argued from time to time and had our moments, but for the most part we were on the same page spiritually and emotionally. Two peas in a pod. Let's put a peg there—we will return.

Because I Said So

In the book of Ecclesiastes, Solomon was inspired to say twenty-nine times, "There is nothing new under the sun." What does that mean? That is a great description of our world—everything from the sun downward.

What else can this phrase mean? There isn't anything new in life. What goes around comes around. People still deal with jobs, marriages, and children as they did at the beginning of time. The Middle Ages rocked with problems just as much as we do in this twenty-first century.

As I have grown older, I have discovered that we can also say, "There is nothing new in life and in the church." God has not changed. He has told us so in Malachi 3:6, "For I, the Lord, do not change." And problems in the church still abound in this century as they did in the first century. I remember Mom's wise observation, "Becky, 99.99 percent of the time, the problems in the church have to do with authority." She was so right. Since Adam, humanity has struggled with God's "because I said so."

People don't basically change either, and what promoted Adam and Eve's downfall in the Garden of Eden continues to promote mankind's downfall today. Sin isn't new. Temptation isn't new either. The same pitfalls that caused Adam and Eve to lose Paradise on earth—the lust of the flesh and the lust of the eyes and the pride of life (1 John 2:16)—still have the same power to separate us from God and destroy our relationship with Him some six thousand years since Eden. Satan is alive and well.

That is not news. You already know it. Mom and I surely knew this. But it seemed to me that whenever we were discussing problems in the world and in the church, bemoaning the issues Christians have with involvement, commitment to the Lord, loving one's husband, and raising children, we continually perceived that the Christian woman's role was as crucial as it had ever been. We were not alone in our quest for answers for the role of the softer sex in God's scheme of things. Our world was asking questions too.

Surely my mom and I were not the first to wonder what God expects of women. Most women ask the same age-old questions: Where do I fit in this life? What is my role? What does God want of me? What is a Christian woman to do for Him in this current age?

And once again, Mom and I would find ourselves turning to the instructions Paul was inspired to write to Titus. It certainly is a given that God knew that His daughters across the ages would desperately need His words, His advice, and His divine instructions for living successful, peaceful, and pleasing lives for Him. Hence, He so graciously and kindly gave us chapter 2 of the letter to Titus.

Everybody Gets Instructions

Before we plunge into the depths of this marvelous chapter, let's stop and realize a very important factor: Paul gives Titus instructions for godly living to *all* age groups: older men, young men, older women, and young women. The Supreme Author speaks to all ages. Where else in the Bible does the Father explicitly do this? Once again God shows that He is fair and just in having instructions for all, male and female, who desire to please Him. A male chauvinist, God is not! But here is the real challenge for Christians: How many of us have read and pondered this amazing chapter? Trust me, God speaks to all of us here. No one gets a free pass.

⟩⟩⟩ PAUSE AND PONDER ⟨⟨⟨

Read Titus 2, Proverbs 31, and Ephesians 5:22–33.

Guidebook for Precious Women

When I was a young mom in the '70s, our country was embroiled in the Woman's Movement. Women were burning their underwear and constantly demonstrating in the streets. Mom and I were intrigued by these women, but we simply did not agree with them. So it was back to the Bible—the authority for everything. We continually sought God's Word to see what He had to say, as His say was final in our lives.

> We studied God's plans for His women to evaluate our progress and standing.

Titus 2 became a well-worn chapter in the pages of our hearts, mainly because we knew God had all the answers to the questions we were asking. (Read 2 Peter 1:3.) God's will was our will. However, we felt varied pressures from the world, friends, and even sisters who wanted nothing to do with what God said and everything to do with what their own hearts desired. So we would return once again to Titus 2, Proverbs 31, and Ephesians 5 and study God's plan for His women and evaluate our progress and standing. The above passages were our standard—our "how to" and "go to" in the "Christian Woman's Guidebook"—tucked inside God's marvelous Bible.

What would I have done without Mom's help in my pursuit of being a woman of God? Without her guidance and encouragement, I probably would have become a completely different Christian than the ol' Beck I know so well today. I'm still a flawed little sheep, but I am blessed because Mom showed fearless courage and persistence. She went the second mile to see that her children knew the importance of knowing God, His Word, and His commandments. She wanted only what all of us moms want: She wanted her children to make it to heaven.

That is why this God-given connection between mothers and daughters is so important. But it doesn't stop there. Please hear me out on this: This all-important connection does not have to be between blood relatives because God has given us many mother-daughter relationships with those who need us. And we need them.

Why This Book?

Mom was compelled to share Bible teaching about this ideal Christian woman in her book from 1986, *Precious Are God's Plans.* It has long been my desire for us women to re-examine and ponder timeless principles she wrote long ago. Many of you have inquired about her books and lessons. As her daughter, I wanted to add selections of her words to this book. You will find them easy to recognize because of the special treatment. Please, please, take your time with this study. Don't rush. Let the passages written to Titus change your life.

I pray that God will help me to help you. Titus 2 is a difficult passage for many women to read and heed. So I ask you, "What will you do with it, my sister? I pray that God will help me to help you. Will you keep an open mind?"

Motivation of Love

I have always loved God. I have never wanted to disappoint Him, but I know I have. I have always wanted to please Him and obey Him, but I know that many times I have done the opposite of what He wanted me to do. God is very real to me. He is the only one who knows me through and through. He is alive and well, and I know that He loves me. The Bible tells me so. And I know that He wants me to love Him and do His will, not mine.

I also realize that I am human, and that humans sin: "For all have sinned and fall short of the glory of God" (Rom. 3:23). But praise God, we can be forgiven of those sins because of Jesus' sacrifice.

PAUSE AND PONDER

Recite John 3:16. Read Romans 5:8 and 1 John 4:7–10. How are these passages linked? In your Bible, underline the common words or phrases.

Daily Bible Study Is a Must!

To be raised by Christian parents is the biggest blessing any child can realize! If you were so blessed, my sister, you ought to get down on your knees and thank God for it every single day! Not everybody gets that blessing.

In our home, God's Word was, and continues to be, the final authority for everything for our family—daily lives, spiritual lives, and the lives the future holds. God was in charge of the Fowler home, and if God said it, that was it! No questions asked. God ruled!

From an early age, my parents encouraged me to begin a daily Bible reading routine. As I reflect on this, I am so grateful that they knew the importance of reading words from the mouth of God every single day. Do you have a Bible-reading plan for yourself and your family?

Do we always recognize the importance, the profoundness, and the power in the following passage written by an inspired Paul to a young Timothy?

> All Scripture is inspired by God and profitable for teaching, for reproof, for correction, for training in righteousness; so that the man of God [or woman of God] may be adequate, equipped for every good work (2 Tim. 3:16–17).

Precious Plans for Precious Women

This is one of the most important passages in the entire Bible, and yet few Christians can tell you where it is found. How sad. This verse is our foundation. It tells others how seriously we take the Bible. This verse reveals who we are and why we follow God every day. Our Christian walk begins with this passage.

The Scriptures are inspired from the mouth of God, and they have the power to teach us, rebuke us, straighten us out, and teach us to do right things. Why? So we can climb the ladder of success, fame, and riches? No! So we can be glamorous and a trendsetter? No! God has given us the Bible so we can live like Him, look like Him, and be equipped to work for Him. Memorize 2 Timothy 3:16–17, my sister. Say it over and over. Remember, it tells you why you are what you are. It is your identity, and it is mine.

PAUSE AND PONDER

Read 2 Timothy 3:16–17 again. Ask yourself, "Is this verse my foundation for daily Bible study? How can I enhance my time with God's Word?

Power to Change

On the day of Pentecost two thousand years ago, Jews gathered from all over the world and asked the Spirit-filled apostles this question: "Brethren, what shall we do?" (Acts 2:37). Down through the ages, men and women still ask, "What do I need to do for forgiveness of my sins? How can I be saved? How can I make things right with God?"

God always tells His creation how to please Him, obey Him, and be saved. God never leaves us in the dark about our salvation. That is what we desire, isn't it? To be saved? Then where do we go for our answers? To the Bible every single time.

Peter was inspired to write to the early church: "Seeing that His divine power has granted to us everything pertaining to life and godliness, through the true knowledge of Him who called us by His own glory and excellence" (2 Pet. 1:3). *Everything* is the key word here. May we never forget that the Bible has all the answers to all the questions in this life. Once again, how good God is to us to give us this marvelous Book.

Why? Because the Bible has the power to change any of us, from the hardened criminal and the hardest of hearts to the kindest of humans.

⇛⇛ PAUSE AND PONDER ⇚⇚

Read Romans 1:16 and underline it in your Bible. How do you show that you are not ashamed of the gospel?

The Greek word for power in Romans 1:16 is *dunamis*, from which we get the word "dynamite." *Dunamis* means strength, power, ability. Now girls, we understand all these definitions, and we understand how mighty the gospel is, especially after reading Acts 2. On that day of Pentecost, Peter preached the first gospel sermon, culminating in the story of Jesus, His death, burial, and resurrection. What happened? A show of power like none other in history. The gospel changed the world! Nothing has been the same or ever will be. Why? Because it was all God's plan. *Dunamis* surely is the right word for the gospel.

> *He never forces us to keep His commandments.*

It is up to us to decide how badly we want to live eternally with the Lord. How important is heaven to us? We can love God and obey His powerful Word, or we can walk away and reject Him altogether. He never forces us to keep His commandments. That is entirely up to us.

God's love for you and me and the whole world is indescribable and unfathomable. It is His earnest desire that no one be lost. Isn't that what 2 Peter 3:9 says? "The Lord is not slow about His promise, as some count slowness, but is patient toward you, not wishing for any to perish but for all to come to repentance."

How kind, merciful, and compassionate Jehovah God is! But we will never know Him or His plan for us if we only read excerpts from His marvelous Word. We must read all of it!

Someone has said, "God didn't give us scripture to scare us. God gave us scripture to prepare us." Open up the book, my sisters, prepare yourselves and find the treasures there.

The Satan Factor

How can we have any biblical discussion without acknowledging the presence of Satan? God doesn't tell us everything about Satan. He doesn't have to. But what we do know is definitely disturbing and fearful.

Recently a preacher and I were having a conversation about Satan and why he was thrown out of heaven. Remember Jesus commenting to His apostles in Luke 10:18: "I was watching Satan fall from heaven like lightning"?

My preacher friend made this interesting observation about a possible reason Satan the angel turned into Satan the devil: "He was jealous and angry. Satan, or Lucifer, was outstanding in the angel world and was a shining star! He loved his status. When he found out that God was going to create mankind and give humans minds to think and the freedom of choice, he just couldn't handle it. Man was going to be created in the image of God and have a relationship with God, and that was more than Satan could bear. He was jealous."

My preacher friend's opinion does make sense, but we must remember that it is just his opinion. God has not given us the details about what all went on in heaven—He doesn't have to! Just consider this theory for a moment. Examine the creation account in Genesis. The first appearance we have of the devil is not during the forming of the firmament or the creation of the animals and birds, but after Adam and Eve had taken their first breaths.

It is while the first couple are enjoying their time in the Garden of Eden and taking care of all their responsibilities that Satan sneakily slithers in. Why then? Could it be that his sudden exit from heaven had just occurred? Now Satan's mission completely revolved around destroying God's human creation. This was his immediate objective, and it has never changed. From the first two humans in the beginning to the seven billion now on the earth, Satan's focus has never changed: he is after you and me.

Here we are, some six thousand years since Creation, and Satan is still as evil, murderous, and vengeful as he has been from day one. Think about it: Satan is jealous of us. God gives us second chances, but the devil will never get a second chance. He hates anything holy, and nothing is too evil for him to use to ensnare us and draw us to his side. He wants us. He delights in tempting us with sinful thoughts and deceitful lifestyles. He continually parades sexual temptations before our eyes and pulls our hearts and minds to dwell on him. The lure of illicit sex is one of Satan's powerful ploys.

The very last thing Satan wants is for us to read and study Titus 2. He wants us to serve him. And don't forget, he wants our children. They are his prey.

The Christian and Satan

When we study Jesus' temptation in the wilderness in Matthew 4 and Luke 4, let's ask ourselves, "Who won that round between Jesus and Satan?" Jesus did, of course, and would win any round to come. With the words, "It is written," Jesus stood in the presence of Satan and then quoted words breathed by God. You and I can do the very same thing. We can say, "It is written," and defeat any temptation Satan has in mind for us. However, we must have scripture in our hearts and minds, and this happens only one way, when you and I *know* scripture—by reading and studying it.

There is a big difference between reading and studying. It all revolves around two words: time and desire. When you take the time to dig deep, study and learn, and ask questions, then you will grow and mature in the faith. Just like in cartoons, a light will go on in your head as you begin to dig into the Word of God, and it is absolutely thrilling! You will become a pearl seeker. Jesus makes all of us this promise in the

Sermon on the Mount: "Blessed are those who hunger and thirst for righteousness, for they shall be satisfied" (Matt. 5:6). When we hunger and thirst for God and His Word, we will get our answers. God will see to it. As we devour His Word, God becomes our source for all things: our hope and our deliverer in this life. "God is our refuge and strength, a very present help in trouble" (Ps. 46:1).

PAUSE AND PONDER

Find these four versions of the Bible to compare 2 Timothy 2:15: KJV, NASB, NKJV, and ESV. Which do you like best? Write that one on an index card and read it aloud every day for one week.

Am I a Worker or a Shirker?

For years I never noticed the word *workman* or *worker* in 2 Timothy 2:15. It takes a lot of work to become an excellent student of the Word. But it is a must that Christians handle the Word of God correctly. Can we make a mistake in interpreting the Scriptures? Oh, yes, we can.

For instance, I have heard of a person who thought Matthew 18:9, instructing us to pluck out our eye if it causes us to stumble, meant that we should literally tear out an offending eye. Another person felt that the only place to pray was in one's closet, a literal interpretation of Matthew 6:6. Neither person was drawing out the meaning of the scripture. We must look at passages, taking the time to study and research the real meaning. That is called "accurately handling the word of truth."

PAUSE AND PONDER

Reflect on an instance in which you or someone else misinterpreted a passage of God's Word. How can this be avoided?

What Does God Want?

These things are foundational as to why we Christians do the things we do, why we treat the Bible the way we do, and why we are so passionate about our Father in heaven. It is our earnest desire to "speak where the Bible speaks and be silent where the Bible is silent."

When God tells us what He wants of women, I sit up and take note! After all, He is speaking to four groups in Titus 2: old men, old women, young women, and young men. When I read the book of Titus, I want to know the circumstances surrounding this epistle and what was on God's mind.

But above all things, I want to know what God wants and expects of me, ol' Beck. If it was important enough for God to breathe His words about women into Paul's pen, then it is of utmost urgency that I stop and handle this passage correctly! I don't want to disobey God.

Several years ago, there was a very popular question passed around in spiritual circles: "What would Jesus do?" It still puts challenges and problems into the proper perspective of being Christlike. Don't we all hold up Jesus as the supreme example to follow? Of course we do. Consider Jesus' marvelous words in John 8:29: "And He who sent Me is with Me; He has not left Me alone, for I always do the things that are pleasing to Him."

Jesus was the Son of God, God in the flesh. So girls, if Jesus always did what was pleasing to God, why can't we do that also? Why can't we strive to please our Father in all things, especially in the qualities He has put forth for us? This is where Titus 2 comes into play. I want to please my Father, and I always will. I know you do too.

Get to Know Titus

Here's an assignment for you! Find out Titus' background, his surroundings, and his nature. Where is Titus when he receives Paul's letter? Titus is referred to thirteen times in the New Testament, so find those verses and examine them. They have a lot to say about this fine young Christian. Titus had to be outstanding, dedicated, and knowledgeable for Paul to have entrusted him with so many responsibilities. However, God never tells us if Titus was married. But let's remember that to this unusual (perhaps young) missionary, the Father gives some of the most profound instructions a Christian woman can ever know, can ever obey, or can ever realize. Just stop and think about it: The task God laid on Titus' shoulders was certainly immense and absolutely essential. Titus' importance in every Christian woman's life is huge.

PAUSE AND PONDER

Find and record the thirteen times the name Titus is mentioned in the New Testament.

As you examine the Titus passages, ask yourself, "What is the Father saying to us women?" Also pray, "Thank You, God, for giving to courageous Titus these guidelines for women. We appreciate his love for You, the Father, and for Your precious women!"

A WOMAN'S PRAYER

Dear Father in heaven, we thank You for loving us and creating us. Thank You for the plans You have in mind for us. O Lord, please help us to work those plans with joy, knowing that we are pleasing You. And that is all that matters. Help us to be good daughters who obey You and honor Your Word. We love You so much. In Jesus' name, Amen."

THOUGHT QUESTIONS

1. Why do you believe the Bible is the inspired Word of God?
2. Are you a daily Bible reader? Give an example of two ways you will improve your daily study. How will you accomplish that?
3. Why did you become a Christian?
4. Quote a scripture that you memorized this past week.

♪ Song: "Wonderful Words of Life"

Insights

You Are Unique

"You never outgrow the need for a mother." What accurate words! I heard them on many occasions, spoken by my mother. Throughout my childhood and adult years, Mom spoke regularly of how much she missed her own mother. At the tender age of nine, she lost her to a debilitating sickness. Being the oldest of three children, Mom shouldered numerous responsibilities to help the family and a heartbroken father.

I cannot imagine what kind of loneliness, emptiness, and confusion a little girl could experience. Mom, of course, knew all about the love of a parent, but not the love of a mother. And she yearned for it as long as she lived.

Women are special. Of course, men are too. God created both: "God created man in His own image, in the image of God He created him; male and female He created them" (Gen. 1:27). Eve was not an afterthought or Plan B. God knew all along that Adam would need a mate, a helper suitable to supply all his needs.

It's interesting that each day of creation ended with "and God saw that it was good." This phrase is used after day one all the way through day five. Then Genesis 1:27 tells us that God created man and then woman, and verse 31 records these words at the end of the sixth day: "And God saw all that He had made, and behold, it was very good."

Of course it was very good! Day six was the best day yet! Man was created, and then woman was created—very good!

> God made the stronger first, and then, in His divine wisdom, He made the weaker, the one who would always need to be encircled. The word *husband* means the "house-binder," the encircler. Just as God made the grass before He made the beast, so He made man before the woman, and then child. Wouldn't you love to have seen Eve? Just imagine her beauty! Wouldn't you love to have seen Adam's face when he saw this woman, fashioned by the hands of God! How happy that wedding day! And what a wonderful place to spend your honeymoon! God did not give Adam a child for a companion. Children are wonderful, exciting, and fill a very needed place in our lives, but they cannot supply what is lacking in man. God did not make another man for Adam. Another man would have removed some of the loneliness, but would still not have been able to supply all the needs. Woman's very femininity, her perceptions, and her tenderness are desirable qualities to a man. We know that whatever was lacking in Adam was supplied by Eve, for God made a helper suitable for him.[2]

One of the things I love most about God is that He cares about women. He loves us! He never treats a woman as a second-class citizen. Men may do that, but not God. He loves all of His creation and has certainly given men the position of leadership in the home and in the church, and I am eternally thankful for that. Believe me, I do not want to be in charge of either one.

But it is the woman who is the heart of the home and the church. God has made her more sensitive, more intuitive, soft as silk and strong as iron—but above all, more nurturing. She may be the weaker vessel (1 Pet. 3:7 KJV), but she certainly has many strengths that a man lacks.

Oh, I know someone wants to argue the nurturing part. But consider the animals and you will see it is the female who feeds, fosters, and fusses over the young for the most part. Please note that I did not make the claim that the male did absolutely nothing to raise the young because he is certainly in the picture, helping very powerfully. But it is the female that God has chosen to be the key player here.

Why? Because the male is to provide and protect, and the female is to take care of the nest—the home. That concept assuredly began when Adam and Eve were banished from the Garden.

Have you ever wondered what would have happened if Adam and Eve had not fallen that horrible day in the Garden? Can we ask that question? Hasn't it ever crossed your mind? If sin had never occurred in the beginning, where would we be now? (Most likely, someone would have stepped over the line along the way and transgressed God's law!)

God had appointed Adam and Eve as caretakers in a paradise unparalleled. They had it made in the shade, literally, with God providing for their every need. But Satan deceived Eve. She tasted the forbidden fruit and then gave the fruit to Adam who also ate it. Suddenly the creation took a nosedive. Everything went terribly wrong the day Evil walked in. Innocence left the Garden, and Sin set up housekeeping.

> *[God] never treats a woman as a second-class citizen.*

Eve was the first sinner. No matter how you try to look at this, it still is hard to accept. At least it is for me. The woman was the first to break God's law—not the man. First John 2:16 springs to life as we contemplate Mother Eve: "For all that is in the world, the lust of the flesh and the lust of the eyes and the boastful pride of life, is not from the Father, but is from the world."

She looked at the fruit, desired the fruit, believed Satan's lies about the fruit and dying, and stepped over the line. That was the day she started to die. And the same goes for Adam, the first man.

Evicted from the Garden, Adam worked hard for a living, farming in the heat and dust, among thorns and thistles. All men have since struggled continually with God's thorns and thistles. And Eve? Her punishment was pain in childbirth, and all women suffer this too.

God understood the temptation scene, all the ins and outs, all that was said, and the naïve emotions swirling in her head. God understood Eve. He also understood Adam. He knew His creation very well.

Another thing to wonder: What kind of people were Adam and Eve? Were they kind, loving, outstanding, and full of integrity? We don't know, do we? We never see them once telling others about Almighty God and His power and love for mankind, even though they had walked and talked with God personally. One thing is evident. Neither of them is mentioned in the Hebrews 11 Hall of Faith and Fame! Hebrews 11 lists those we hold up as marvelous examples of faith to emulate. Think about that for a moment or two. There are many theories as to why their names are not mentioned in Hebrews 11. But the fact is that God chose not to mention them as being people with outstanding faith in Him.

Some six thousand years have passed since Eve walked on this earth, and she is still a hot topic! I believe she will always be so—at least among us girls.

You are unique, my sister. Unique and loved. So was Mother Eve. Never forget that. God made you special, and that in itself should give you confidence. Each day is a new day full of opportunities to encourage others, to be salt and light, to learn and grow, and to start all over again.

Do something every day to draw you closer to God. Wouldn't the world be a wonderful place if we all took this to heart? Wouldn't the church, our spiritual family, experience more growth, strength, and kindness in its midst if we were more determined to seek the Lord daily? And wouldn't our own precious physical family finally realize the love and closeness we women long for?

Never forget that God has a plan for you and me. I don't know about you, but I am going to work His plan with all my heart, with all my soul and with all my strength.

"For I know the plans that I have for you," declares the LORD, "plans for welfare and not for calamity to give you a future and a hope. Then you will call upon Me and come and pray to Me, and I will listen to you. You will seek Me and find Me when you search for Me with all your heart" (Jer. 29:11–13).

Take hold of the life God has given you and love yourself. God doesn't make any junk. Believe in yourself and the specific tailor-made journey the Father has personally given you to travel. Obey the gospel of Jesus, my sister, and you will find a life worth living. Stay the course, for a life lived without God just doesn't make any sense at all. Don't you think Eve had to learn that lesson too?

Becky and her mom in Rome, 1980

CHAPTER 2

You Are the PRECIOUS Woman

"Older women likewise are to be reverent in their behavior, not malicious gossips nor enslaved to much wine, teaching what is good" (Tit. 2:3).

Jump In!

The book of Philippians is often called the "Epistle of Joy," because it focuses on finding joy regardless of circumstances. The book of Titus could be called the "Epistle of Practical Living." Here is a book where the "rubber meets the road" when it comes to living the Christian life. God sets forth the qualities He desires all His children to possess. For that reason alone, Titus should be a favorite for us all. James Burton Coffman says, "The epistle to Titus is an epistle on the practical side of the Christian living."[3]

Not only was Paul inspired by God to write Titus and give him instructions to help the church in Crete, but to "set in order" the workings of the church—the appointing of elders. First things first were on Paul's agenda in writing this letter, as we read Paul's greeting to Titus, and then immediately Paul launches into the matter of the qualifications of elders. Paul wasted little time in addressing what the Christians in Crete needed to hear and do.

It is very important for students of the Bible to know this important epistle called Titus. Barclay has these amazing words to describe Titus:

> The pastoral epistles, as 1 and 2 Timothy and Titus are called, have been undeservedly neglected by ordinary readers of the Bible. They are of the greatest interest, for no letters in the New Testament give such a vivid picture of the growing church. In them we see the problems of a Church which is a little island of Christianity in a sea of paganism; and in them we see as nowhere else the first beginnings of the ministry of the church . . . But the fact is that just because they were written when the Church was becoming an institution, they speak most directly to our situation and condition.[4]

What Were Cretans Like?

The preacher Titus had quite a task! Living on the island of Crete would be a challenge for any Christian. The Cretans were heavily involved in all kinds of immorality. They were not known for their integrity or compassion. Instead, they were a disreputable bunch.

> One of themselves, a prophet of their own, said, "Cretans are always liars, evil beasts, lazy gluttons." This testimony is true. For this reason, reprove them severely so that they may be sound in the faith, not paying attention to Jewish myths and commandments of men who turn away from the truth (Tit. 1:12–14).

Notice the comments below by David Lipscomb regarding specific sinful behavior of the Cretans.

> This terrible estimate of the Cretan character [lying] is amply borne out by the testimony of many profane writers. The words "to Cretanize," or to play the part of a Cretan, is synonymous with "to deceive" or "to utter a lie." Not only were they liars but were gross and sensual, living in animalism and for it. All men may be called "beasts" who attend to their animal appetites as a means of

gratification rather than relief. He who seeks happiness from his senses rather than his spiritual nature is no better than a beast . . . Their gluttony made them dull, heavy, and indolent. These sins were true of the Cretans generally in their unregenerate state; but sins prevalent among a people before they become Christians will possibly be their besetting sins after they become such . . . The Christians were still tempted into the sins which these qualities would lead."[5]

In chapter 2 we learn that women were prone to drink: "nor enslaved to much wine" (Tit. 2:3). Evidently there was a real problem in Crete. David Lipscomb said, "The women of Crete were given to wine drinking. Observe the fitness of the phrase 'enslaved.' The drunkard is thoroughly the slave of his appetite."[6]

As notorious drinkers, Paul told Titus to "reprove them severely." Imagine Titus' telling the church strongly and harshly that they were living in sin, and not sparing any feelings in doing so. I don't think Titus was everyone's favorite preacher, do you? Yet God inspired Paul to tell Titus to teach, reprove, and rebuke those Christians whose lifestyle reflected lying, sensual living, and drinking. There were definite problems in the Cretan churches, and God wanted them stopped immediately. Examine these first two chapters of Titus again, and notice that God never minces words about His children's behavior.

⟶⟶⟶ PAUSE AND PONDER ⟵⟵⟵

Take a moment and brainstorm what life in Crete was like for the church. What topics might Titus have preached about?

How to Be a Real Christian

In Titus 2 we see the personal qualities God desires all Christians to embrace as they walk this walk of faith. It is here that we see the real Christian—young and old.

> But as for you, speak the things which are fitting for sound doctrine. Older men are to be temperate, dignified, sensible, sound in faith,

in love, in perseverance. Older women likewise are to be reverent in their behavior, not malicious gossips nor enslaved to much wine, teaching what is good, so that they may encourage the young women to love their husbands, to love their children, to be sensible, pure, workers at home, kind, being subject to their own husbands, so that the word of God will not be dishonored. Likewise urge the young men to be sensible; in all things show yourself to be an example of good deeds, with purity in doctrine, dignified, sound in speech which is beyond reproach, so that the opponent will be put to shame, having nothing bad to say about us (Tit. 2:1–8).

Jump in the Deep End!

We are plunging into the deep end of the pool, girls. So let's jump in and see what God has to say! As we begin this study, may we consider the important fact that Paul wanted Titus to urge four groups of Christians: The older men, the older women, and the younger women and the younger men. Read more closely and you will see who is charged to encourage the younger women. It is not Titus; not the older men; not the younger men. It is the older women who are to help the young women. How smart God is in this! After all, my sisters, stop and think: Whom do you want to encourage you and instruct you on how to act, live, and run your home—an older man or a younger man? Neither one! Burton Coffman notes, "Significantly, the elders were not entrusted with the training of young married women, a function that pertained to the godly older women in the congregation."[7]

What does *train* mean in Titus 2? According to Carl Spain, "The word for *train* means to school them and encourage them in matters of good sense, wise discretion, and sober conduct, especially in relationship to husband and children."[8]

How much easier it is to take instructions on home, family, and personal Christ-filled attributes from an older loving woman than from a man, young or old. (Titus had plenty to do without having to counsel the young women. He must have breathed a sigh of relief when he learned the older women were to teach the younger women.) Don't you want a wise, older woman who has "been there, done that and got the T-shirt"? A woman who has walked in your shoes and survived? God knew what all women would need because He designed us. He knows all the ins and outs of His handwork called "woman," and He knows what makes her tick. Come to think of it, God is the only one who knows what makes us tick.

We must be wise when it comes to helping other women and their relationship problems. It can be very dangerous for a Christian woman with marital problems to seek the counsel of an elder or preacher or brother in the faith. Satan looks for opportunities to destroy marriages, and in my life experience, the stories of affairs and adulteries in the church occur frequently when a vulnerable sister is advised by a Christian brother. Wise is the congregation where women are counseled by a Titus 2 woman. Oh, the homes and families that have been destroyed by Satan's temptations in counseling matters.

Let's examine Mom's thoughts on what God wants an older woman to do.

⋙ MOM SAYS ⋘

*T*itus, you encourage the older women, who have God's qualifications for teaching, to teach the younger Christian women what is lacking in their young lives.

> Older women likewise are to be reverent in their behavior, not malicious gossips, nor enslaved to much wine, teaching what is good, so that they may encourage the young women to love their husbands, to love their children, to be sensible, pure, workers at home, kind, being subject to their own husbands, so that the word of God will not be dishonored (Tit. 2:3–5).

God, who knows all, knows that love is a decision, a learned art. We learn to love our husbands, our children, and our homes—maybe. We love ourselves instinctively by nature.

If love is learned, who will teach us? If we had a loving mother, we have been blessed. Most people quickly identify true love with motherhood. Mothers sacrifice, deny themselves, and look for their children's good before their own.

However, God knows that a godly woman is one of the best teachers for young Christian women. Many young women have had no godly examples in their upbringing. They come in from the world, from the highways and the hedges. They are eager to learn, yes, but know little about real love.

∾ REVERENT IN THEIR BEHAVIOR

Why should older women be reverent in their behavior? Because a silly woman is a natural part of youth. Foolishness is not only "bound in the heart of a child" (Prov. 22:15 KJV), but also in the hearts of grownups who act immaturely. Have you ever seen a childish bride?

Many young ladies when they marry are unable to cook, clean a house, please a husband or God. When my youngest daughter went off to a Christian college, she was amazed at the mothers who came down every weekend to wash and iron their daughters' clothes! Young married women still giggle, sleep late, and dream of the same things they dreamed of while they were single—pretty clothes, good times, and the opposite sex. Soap operas know that these subjects entice the immature, and they deal hearty portions of the three daily: pretty clothes, good times, and sex. Take these things out of soap operas and there would be no soap!

But when we become a woman—an older Christian woman, especially—we must put away childish things. I remember a class of teenage girls that I taught years ago. Several were seniors in high school, and some of their classmates were soon getting married. The girls were twittering excitedly about marriage and the advantages of being "freed brides" instead of "chained children." I asked them to close their eyes and then said something like this: "How many of you are ready to leave home? Ready for the bridal shower, the wedding, your first apartment, a young man who adores you, and freedom from parental discipline? Ready to leave home and make your own decisions?" Almost every girl eagerly raised her hand.

"Close your eyes once more. Now let your mind go to your mother. How many are ready to swap places with her? Ready to do her work and bear all of her responsibilities? Look at her closet—ready to exchange wardrobes with her? Are you willing to be in subjection to an older man like your father? Are you ready to settle for her entertainments and lack of them? Are you ready to make her sacrifices?"

Not a hand was raised—only sober faces looked at me. I wonder how these girls are doing now as they follow mother's footsteps!

❧ NOT MALICIOUS GOSSIPS

"I know we are not supposed to repeat anything unless it is good, but this is good!" Gossip is so delicious, so interesting, so shocking, so much fun when we are young and, if we are not careful, when we're older. God said older women have to work on this, and He knows us.

But older women, older godly women, should know the danger of gossip and the repercussions that can develop. The end result can be destroyed lives, a family break-up, suicide, divorce, or a lost soul. And the lost soul could be that of a gossiper!

God tells us that a good name is better than riches. Shakespeare says that when you steal a man's purse, you steal trash, but when you steal his good name, you do him irreparable damage. Somehow the Chinese know how to teach their children to live in such a way that they will never dishonor the family name. I wish we could learn that!

Malicious gossip is the worst of all! It hopes to hurt; it does not care what the consequences may be. It enjoys another's misfortune and willfully repeats and embellishes the current story. It does not hesitate to "murder" the reputation of another, even of another child of God.

How can we expect the young women to want to confide in a gossipy old woman who will tell it all? How can they expect help from the tale bearer? "The words of a whisperer are like dainty morsels, and they go down into the innermost parts of the body" (Prov. 18:8).

Older women who are going to be helpful to God must remember how hard it is to be young. They must remember that all of us still sin daily and fall short of the glory of God. They must remember how awful it is not to know the answers that are so easily understood in later life because of practice and lessons learned through trial and error. You can never be an effective counselor if you are easily shocked or cannot remember the sins of your own youth.

> Rejoice, young man, during your childhood, and let your heart be pleasant during the days of young manhood. And follow the impulses of your heart and the desires of your eyes. Yet know that God will bring you to judgment for all these things. So remove grief and anger from your heart and put away pain from your body, because childhood and the prime of life are fleeting (Eccles. 11:9–10).

Good women must be able to see the end of a distressing situation and to know that whatever it is, it could happen to you or yours! How can we expect mercy if we have not been merciful? I have known older Christian women who kept the wedding dates on the calendar to be sure the first baby wasn't born too soon. And I have also seen these same women have this eventually come into their own families.

Mothers and grandmothers make such a mistake when they assure everyone that their offspring would never do such and such. They underestimate the power of Satan and overestimate the strength of their children. Only God knows the scope of the sins we have yet to commit.

Families tend to spread their wings over their own while they are in trouble because "love covers a multitude of sins" (1 Pet. 4:8). The older woman should realize that her love must cover the sins of others, too, especially the sins of the family of God. She should sympathize with the tears and heartbreak of the situation and forget the excitement of the gossip. She must remember, "There go I, but by the grace of God, or my children."

God tells us to weep with those who weep and rejoice with those who rejoice. A scripture that has always helped me at times of family sins or embarrassments or humiliations is found in Ecclesiastes 11:1–2. "Cast your bread on the surface of the waters, for you will find it after many days. Divide your portion to seven, or even to eight, for you do not know what misfortune may occur on the earth."

This scripture is telling us that we had better share what we have with others because we don't know what is ahead of us. Share your love and understanding with seven or eight, and then when you need a friend, someone will reach for you with the same sort of love and understanding that you have shown to others.

RECIPROCATION

I met a stranger in the night, whose lamp had ceased
   to shine;
I paused and let him light his lamp from mine.
A tempest sprung up later on and shook the world
   about.
And when the wind was gone, my lamp was out.
But back to me the stranger came—his lamp was
   glowing fine!
He held the precious flame and lighted mine.

—Lon Woodrum[9]

NOR ENSLAVED TO WINE

This portion of Scripture puzzled me for years. How could any older godly woman who wanted to teach younger women be an alcoholic?

God is a realist. He knows what is going on in His world and in His family, the church. There have always been secret drinkers, and there always will be. Women, because of the double standard, especially want these addictions hidden.

Again, we must find mercy in our hearts for temptations that we don't have. No one can sympathize with another to the extent that is needed until he has had the same temptation. This is why the various support groups for drinking, gambling, and overeating are so successful. A group is saying, "1 know how bad it is because it had or has me hooked."

We, who may be smug about our self-control, may have to give second thoughts about our addictions to Valium or other doctor-given prescriptions. Somehow we are going to have to become "unaddicted." I remember a good woman coming to us for counsel who had been placed on drugs by her psychiatrist. We felt so sorry for her in her innocent predicament. It took a tremendous struggle for her to be freed again, but she made it. And if I remember right, she did it cold turkey.

Women of Bible times had a ready supply of wine at their fingertips. Wine was a way out from the present pain—whatever that pain was. It could have been the loss of a husband's love, the empty nest, boredom, depression, or just sheer loneliness. They didn't have television, a ready supply of reading matter, or telephones.

"Don't do it," God says. "You will cancel out your effectiveness. This is the time that you have to be among the greatest workers in the kingdom. Your husbands are still busy making the living, but you have almost unlimited time to be about your Father's business." As the old song goes, "Let your eyes see the need of workers today."

ஓ But Rather by Good Works

First Timothy 2:10 says, "But rather by means of good works as is proper for women making a claim to godliness." Older women who are making such a claim, you are needed so badly. Where are you?

There are things that need to be said to young Christian women that only you can say effectively. You are a living proof, a testimony, that the young can take to heart. You survived! You are happy and much wiser than you used to be; you've raised good children who are faithful or were when they lived with you; your husband loves you; your children love you; you've survived your heartbreaks; and yet you come to teach with a smile on your face. Come in.

"Help me to be a survivor, too, and to reap the same sort of blessings that God has poured out on you. I want peace and joy and kindness and security and my husband's love and my children's obedience and answers—today!" This is what the younger women are saying.

Maybe the reason they want you to say these things to them is because most women never outgrow their need for a mama. I haven't, and I'm sixty-six. And remember, they say that a woman who will tell her age will tell anything.

> *It is easy to overemphasize the "do nots" and leave undone the "dos."*

Probably, it is easier to hear an older woman teach submission than to hear the young preacher teach the same lesson!

Titus, teach the older woman what she lacks and then encourage her to go to the young women who want her and need her. They are tied in the house with noise and young children and earaches and bed-wetting! God knows what is needed, and He spells it out for the good of all.

⁊ WHERE ARE THE OLDER WOMEN?

In each generation the body of Christ should be restoring more fully the New Testament church. We must ever be in the process of following the given pattern of perfection laid out in the Scriptures.

Maybe one of the reasons we have not encouraged the older women to teach is because of the restrictions God has placed on women not to take the pulpit. The desire to please God is felt by the church, and so a restriction can cause us to go too far the other way and fail to fulfill the job given to women. It is easy to overemphasize the "do nots" and leave undone the "dos."

There is a place for women to learn and to learn quietly. It has always been a principle of God's both in the Old and the New Testament that the men teach the assemblies. But this should not nullify the teaching of God for older women to teach the younger women. There are as many women to be taught as men, if not more. The older woman has a mind-boggling assignment. She is to be busy helping to instruct the younger Christian women as well as discipling her world.

Christian growth is not the struggle to become the kind of person we think God wants us to be, but a surrender of our bodies, all our faculties, our right to ourselves, to God that He may make us and mold us into the image of His Son, that through us His life and love and grace might flow.

—Rick Halverson

If the Spirit is working in our lives through His Holy Word, then we should want to please our Father and should have the faith to know that His way works. It is in dying to self that we can become the workers that God desires us to be. Jesus set the perfect example to us all in obedience when He said, "Not my will, but Thine be done."

It is immaturity and lack of faith that make us petulantly say, "But I don't want it that way."

It is in our faults and failings, not in our virtues, that we touch one another and find sympathy.

—Jerome K. Jerome[10]

∾ Let's Plan Ladies Days!

We spend hundreds of dollars yearly to have preachers hold special meetings for the church. It is hoped that they, too, will touch our souls and renew our minds and activate our service for the Lord. They do well!

But why can't we be just as concerned to have our women taught by women? Women are sociable creatures who naturally gravitate to spending time together. A church with dedicated women will send out waves of good throughout the whole body of Christ. Husbands will be more loved, submitted to, and appreciated. Children will be more loved and more loveable, more obedient, more like Timothy when they are grown. Homes will be happier, lovelier, more hospitable, cleaner, more peaceful, and more anxious to be returned to. Women will mature faster, and the fruit of the Spirit will be more noticeable in their lives. God will be more glorified in His daughters.

Why don't we encourage such wonders? It could be for several reasons or combination of reasons.

We may not know what Titus teaches.

We may not believe it.

We may fear that women should be content with things as they are, lest harm come from increased activities.

No doubt, there is the probability that somewhere, sometime, mistakes will be made, but mistakes are made in every phase of proclaiming the Word. And women teaching women is pleasing God by our obedience to His Word. God's way works, and faith believes it. Thankfully, many churches have added ladies' events in their budgets; the benefits warrant it. God's money should be used to carry out God's teachings.

ꙮ Our Work Is before Us

Let us turn to the list of subjects and qualities that will increase awareness in young women so that they can consciously see their needs. God fashioned women with His own hands, and it increases our faith to read His list of what we need to work on. The Creator knows and loves and understands the created. May we trust our souls and bodies to His care and instructions as we open the following chapters.

Caution—Yellow Tape!

We have quite the challenge before us, my sisters. God inspired Paul to tell Titus to admonish the older women to focus on seven—that perfect number—attributes God wants younger women to have (Tit. 2:4–5). Coffman puts it this way:

> There are seven qualities to be instilled in the younger women, two mentioned in this verse, five in the next. They are: (1) husband-lovers, (2) children-lovers, (3) sober-minded, (4) chaste, (5) workers at home, (6) kind, and (7) in subjection to their own husbands.[11]

Before we start paddling around in this pool of seven qualities, there is something very profound that we must take to heart. Notice that God gives the qualities that an older woman should have in her own life before she assists a younger woman in her life. Does this ring a bell somehow inside your head? It should. What did Jesus say?

> Why do you look at the speck that is in your brother's eye, but do not notice the log that is in your own eye? Or how can you say to your brother, "Let me take the speck out of your eye," and behold, the log is in your own eye? You hypocrite, first take the log out of your own eye, and then you will see clearly to take the speck out of your brother's eye (Matt. 7:3–5).

Now, tell me, girls, how in the world can an older Christian woman have any good effect on anyone if her own life is a total mess? How in all good conscience can I sit down and tell another woman how to love her husband if I am known to be a lousy wife, not to mention being a loud-mouth old gossip? How can I be taken seriously if I am an ugly example of a godly woman?

Consider the older woman. What does she need to look like? It is crucial for us to examine all the qualities we older women are to have before we can give out advice. Be sure to note the quality of being reverent. The King James Version translates this "as becometh holiness." I have known some wonderful Christian women who were holy and reverent. If they had come to me, I would have been "all ears" to anything they had to say, even if it were criticism, because I respected them and saw their attitude toward our Father. Many years ago, Adam Clarke wrote these words about the behavior of the older women:

> That they be in their dress, gait, and general deportment, such as their holy calling requires; that they be not like the world, but like the Church, decent without, and adorned with holiness within.[12]

I am an older woman now. I must make sure that the log Jesus taught about is out of my own eye before I can help anyone. If a younger woman cannot see Christ living in me, then my words are going to be futile. Why should she listen to anything I have to say? Put yourself in the younger woman's shoes as she views you and your reputation. What is going on in her head as you enter her home and sit down on her couch, ready to disperse wisdom? How wise God is to tell the older woman to be living right before she can help another woman to live right—right?

Do the Math —It Is 7/11!

By the way, if you are doing the math here, the older woman is to help the younger woman with seven qualities she needs to put in her life. The older woman—if she has been married and raised children—should already have those seven qualities and four more as well. God tells us that the older woman is to be reverent, not a gossip, not enslaved to wine, and teaching what is good. If you add all this up, the special older woman is to have eleven solemn, godly attributes in her own life before she can encourage and help train a younger woman. To say that God is seriously descriptive about what He wants is an understatement.

> *Live right before you help another to live right.*

⟶≫≫ **PAUSE AND PONDER** ≪≪⟵

Older woman, ask yourself: "Do I have all eleven qualities? Which ones do I need to work on?"

The Titus 2 Woman

The older woman does not have to be ancient with one foot in the grave. She also does not have to be a woman who has been married and raised children. She may be an older single woman who still is reverent and wise. We are all older than someone, aren't we? Of course we are. The main point is that we women need to be sensitive to others and see the needs in the sisters around us. There definitely is a ministry here for older women in the church.

Look in the Mirror

As we end this chapter, let's look at what James, the half-brother of Jesus, wrote:

> For if anyone is a hearer of the word and not a doer, he is like a man who looks at his natural face in a mirror; for once he has looked at himself and gone away, he has immediately forgotten what kind of person he was. But one who looks intently at the perfect law, the law of liberty, and abides by it, not having become a forgetful hearer but an effectual doer, this man will be blessed in what he does (James 1:23–25).

Do you and I want the younger women to love us and have respect for us? If so, let's examine ourselves. Let's look honestly at our spiritual image in the mirror of His Word. Let's take a long, long look. If we need to make adjustments, then let's do it and do it now! If there ever were going to be a description of what ol' Beck was in this life, it is my fervent prayer that my brethren would say, "You know, Becky was a godly, wise woman." And not, "You know, that Becky sure was a worldly busybody."

All Christians should be in the Word, doers of the Word, and living it in front of others. James 1:21 says something we need to remember about God's Word. It is able to save our souls—all souls. Older men. Older women. Younger women. Younger men. That is why we are Christians in the first place. We want to be saved for eternity. We want to get rid of all those dirty sins and pray that God remembers them no more. Heaven is our goal!

Sweet young women, we older women love you and we just want to help. Why? Because we want you to go to heaven—you, your husband, your children, and your family. Please let us in the door so we can help.

⌐ A WOMAN'S PRAYER ⌐

Our dearest Father, please guide us and love us through these passages from Your lips to the women who are so privileged to call You Father. Help us to see what You want and not what we want. It is all about You and not about us. Please help us as we try to be what You want us to be. Please help us to be strong and do the right thing. Please help us to surrender. We love You, Father. Help us. In Jesus' name, Amen.

◆ THOUGHT QUESTIONS ◆

1. Why should you have an older godly woman help you?
2. Would you rather be helped privately or publicly by an older woman? Why?
3. How are you aspiring to be a godly woman?
4. What changes do you need to make?

♪ Song: "Give Me the Bible"

Insights

The Important Orange Book

It has been pure pleasure for me to write about my mom and the many lessons she has taught me through the years. Mom took raising her children very seriously, but she took raising her children *in the Lord* even more seriously. She never let an opportunity slip by with her own family, with the world, or with her spiritual family to impress on them the importance of the Bible. I remember two of these opportunities she had with me that I have shared with you in previous books, both occurring when I was a young mother and Mom was visiting with our family. In those instances, she taught me valuable admonitions about the Lord and His Word.

Today is a little different. You are going to read about an encounter with her that was extremely unpleasant. She was *angry*; she was hot, and I was on her list! (The wrath of Lea Emma, as my Jeff calls it.) No one wanted to be on Lea Fowler's list! Trust me on that. Irish she was. Scottish she was. Red-haired she was. Short fuse—well, let's put it this way: she had no fuse. She was fuseless. Any reprimanding from her usually went like this for me as a child: I goofed. I transgressed a rule. Whap! Instant chastening. Instant discipline. She never waited for Dad to get home! Mom was the fastest draw in the north, south, east, and west when it came to simultaneously grabbing a paddle of sorts and swatting us kids. Somehow her hands found a brush, a flyswatter, a wooden spoon—anything that was closest to her. (Her favorite weapon of choice was a "Bo-Lo" paddle which she purchased at the five-and-dime store, promptly ripped off the tiny ball, and tucked the paddle into her purse.) I never saw it coming—she was that fast! If she had been put to the test, she would have beaten Doc Holliday or Wyatt Earp or any gunslinger hands down. If Lea Emma had been alive and the town marshal in Tombstone, Arizona, in 1881, the only thing the OK Corral would have been known for was parking horses. She was that "fastest"!

Now let me add something of utmost importance. Mom always— and I do mean always—sat me down after any correcting incident, wrapped me in her arms, explained why the spanking occurred, and that, above all things, she loved me no matter what. Always.

I honestly do not think there is anyone alive who truly relishes being "in trouble" with his or her mother. No matter how old you are or how much you have achieved in this life, you know that is true. Presidents, world leaders, and the top names in Fortune 500 companies were once children who definitely had faults and likely received punishments of one kind or another. Put your brain into rewind and relive those memories of scoldings and time-outs, even the spankings. You might agree that you needed the discipline at the time, although the memories can be very uncomfortable.

My parents instructed, taught, and disciplined—and loved their three children. We were three redheaded kids with lots of energy and no brains. (Sorry, Tom and Judy. We just didn't think. Locking Mom in the bathroom comes to mind.) We were typical kids. When I reflect on the words most frequently flowing from my mom's mouth to my ears, I hear: "Your timing is off!" "Stop whining!" "Both of us are going to Fist City and only one of us is coming back!" "Think!" And she was right.

Mom was once visiting Jeff and me when we were newlyweds, living in Georgia in our first little house. She was working on something, a lesson to teach or a spiritual thought to develop. She asked me this very simple question: "Becky, where is your concordance? I need to find a scripture." Simple request but oh, the lesson I was "fixing to" learn.

"The concordance? Where is it?" I asked myself. I looked at Jeff and asked him where it was. It was Greek to him. Literally. He had been a Christian for a while but had no idea what I was talking about.

Jeff and I both flew about the house, searching for any book stash. I knew to look for the orange colored Cruden's Concordance, a gift from Mom and Dad as I left home. I knew what it was. Jeff did not. I just kept whispering urgently to him, "Orange, orange!" I went one way, and Jeff went the other way. At one point I remember seeing him on his knees, digging in the front hall closet where some books and old records were. He was pulling out book after book and asking my mom, "Is this it? Is this it?"

I actually do not remember who found it. All I know is that it was found and things settled down at our little house, but not for long.

Like all the other lessons my mom taught me in that first home of ours, she once more sat me down on the couch. You know, there's a lot to this "sitting down on the couch" stuff. It makes both parties stop. It makes both parties look at one another. And it makes both parties communicate—hopefully.

As I can recall, she said something like this: "Becky, you didn't know where your concordance was. Jeff didn't even know what it was. You did not have it in a special place where you could readily and easily find it."

And then—this I do remember—she looked at me with her eyes narrowed and burrowing deep down into my soul. Then she very sternly said, "Don't. You. Ever. Ever. Let. This. Happen. Again." Funny how a certain tone in my mother's voice could instantly reduce me into a third grader. Sometimes the most valuable lessons in life are painful to learn. And yet, I knew what she was saying, and I knew what else she was saying—two meanings here. I translate it this way:

1. "Becky, a concordance is one of the most necessary books you must have in order to find scriptures and grow your faith. You need it to learn your Bible. Always know where it is!"
2. "Becky, teach Jeff what a concordance is."

I do and I have. Presently, my computer is my concordance. How thankful I am to find a scripture I am searching for in less than ten seconds! If this same scene with Mom had happened today, I would have had to know where the concordance is on the internet. Do you know where to find your concordance?

Please let me help you here, because most people have a computer. Check out blueletterbible.org or biblegateway.com. Keep these tools at your right hand; they are excellent.

Thanks, Mom, for the painful but needful lesson. I know that I needed to learn it. Once more you have exhibited the age-old concept that love and discipline go hand in hand. I will never. Ever. Forget. It.

Becky and her mom, 1983

*Russ and Lea
dating, 1940*

March — 1940

*Lea with Becky
on her wedding
day, 1972*

CHAPTER 3

Love YOUR MAN, Girls

". . . that they may encourage the young women to love their husbands . . ."

*D*on't you think it is interesting that the first thing on God's list of directives for young women is to love their husbands? Perhaps if you or I had been asked what we would have listed first, we would have said, "The children must come first!" But our Father disagrees. The husband has top priority. (Somehow I hear a man's voice in the background, saying, "All right!")

The Father knows us women, His daughters, and how much our hearts are tied to our children and their constant demands. He also knows how easy it is for us to become so absorbed in our offspring's lives that we often overlook God's original role assignment for us as a "help suitable" for our husbands. What about his wants and needs? Often it is difficult for men to adjust to "finding their place" in the family when the babies start arriving and turn a couple's love nest upside down.

Someone has said, "Motherhood is really about accepting the fact that you will be permanently worried for the rest of your life." Do you relate to that? It is certainly true that most women have concern about their children, no matter their ages. But it is also true that we can allow this apprehension to consume us to the point that we shut out our husbands. So let's look at who God wants to be loved first—the husband.

PAUSE AND PONDER

Read Psalm 37:1–5, Philippians 4:6–7, Matthew 6:34, and Proverbs 22:25. What does each verse have in common?

Happy, Happy, Happy

Wouldn't you say that we all want to be happy? Isn't that what you want? Thomas Jefferson, as he drafted the *Declaration of Independence*, considered the pursuit of happiness as a lifetime quest for most people.

And wouldn't you also say that we all want to be loved? Absolutely. In pursuing happiness we embrace falling in love and getting married. We want that; we desire happiness and love. Marianne Williamson once said, "For many, many people, getting married is one of the most important things they will ever do in the pursuit of happiness."[13]

Getting married is what most girls think and dream about from preschool days. By the time girls reach marriageable age, most have mentally planned the wedding, "the dress," the bridesmaid dresses, the venue, and probably the food!

Look at the rising cost of weddings: the locales, the dress, and the honeymoon! The sky is the limit! I saw somewhere that the average cost of a wedding in the U. S. is approximately $34,000 including the engagement ring, ceremony, and reception." And that figure doesn't even include the honeymoon. The TV series *Say Yes to the Dress* is quite an eye opener when it comes to bridal budgets! However, I remember my dad remarking on many occasions, "Girls want a wedding, but they don't want a marriage." You are so right, Dad.

Parents will spend thousands and thousands for their children to have the most lavish wedding of the year. It's a red carpet, petal strewn event! But few thoughts are given to marriage counseling, communication, the budget, or even how to raise the children that will come into the union. All the focus for many couples is concentrated on passion and presentation—the love and the way they think it should look in the wedding album.

But what about the real love between a man and a woman? How many of you remember hearing Tammy Wynette's song "Stand by Your Man"? Look up those lyrics, and you'll agree that truer words were never spoken, for it surely is tough to be a woman. Just ask Eve! And then, it is tough for some women to give all their love to just one man.

God's marriage plan has always been "one man, one woman, one lifetime." Usually, when we women love a man, we love him 'til we die, and there is no doubt about it!

How special is the love between a man and a woman? Well, do you have forty days and forty nights for us to discuss it? Love can make or break you; love can send you soaring to the heavens and can drag you to the depths of torment. It can be the best of the best and the worst of the worst.

Falling in love can be the most thrilling thing you will know in this life, but falling in love with the wrong person can hurl a heart into great remorse and tragedy. Romantic love has been the inspiration for poetry and literature down through the ages. It is the recurring theme with which most songs are obsessed, and Hollywood continually dishes out a steady diet of passion, sex, relationships, and all the complications in between. All in the name of love.

How to Fall in Love

When it comes to serious relationships and affairs of the heart, be careful! In teaching younger women to love their husbands, are single women included? Yes. Singles must tread cautiously because emotions often take over and cloud important issues. Physical attraction and sexual tensions often interfere with the pure relationship two people are trying to develop. A person often marries without really knowing his or her spouse. The "physical" moment surfaces and makes a young man or woman believe that the sexual urges are pure, unadulterated, and authentic love. My mama used to say that those urges were baby-making feelings.

Include these cautions when teaching younger women:

- ✤ *Avoid putting yourself into sexual temptations.* Sexual feelings are very natural and incredibly strong, but God says to run!

- ✤ *Flee immorality.* Every other sin that a man commits is outside the body, but the immoral man sins against his own body (1 Cor. 6:18).

Courting, dating, and time are extremely necessary for two people to become acquainted. It takes time to know one another's likes and dislikes. It takes time to discover personality quirks and differing opinions. There must be disagreements and arguments, for they force a couple to resolve problems. It is good to see the other side of a boyfriend, because when dating one is likely to be on one's best behavior.

That old saying, "Marry in haste and repent in leisure," surely can come back to bite the duo that rushed down the aisle. Take your time. Yes, there are times when a couple simply cannot wait to marry, and God understands that, too. Listen to Paul's admonition in 1 Corinthians 7:9: "But if they do not have self-control, let them marry; for it is better to marry than to burn with passion."

PAUSE AND PONDER

What are some ways a couple can get better acquainted? What should they not do?

Loving vs. Liking

I love old movies. *Shenandoah* is close to my heart. James Stewart, the father, asks his daughter's suitor, "Do you like her?" The young man quickly replies, "Of course I do. I love her!" Stewart replies, "There's some difference between loving and liking."

That difference is called friendship. Oh yes, there must be that "spark" between the man and woman who are courting—unequivocally. However, that spark is able to muddy the water when it comes to assessing a couple's compatibility. Questions that should be asked are: Do we get along with one another? Are we friends? Do we like each other? Do we like the same things? How much do we have in common? Are there any anger issues here? Is this person a Christian?

I once knew an engaged couple who suddenly parted ways. We all wondered what had happened, but neither revealed the reason they had split. Years later I learned that the young man had slapped his fiancée during an argument, and she immediately called the wedding off. Smart girl. Whatever you do, do not ignore violence of any kind—from either party. If your "friend" has the gall to slap you, stop right there. Don't take another step. You will become his punching bag if he can get that wedding band on your finger. And if a young woman has the gall to slap her fiancé, violence will most likely spill over into that marriage, too. It works both ways.

Building a good foundation for a relationship requires time. Get to know one another through wholesome activities. And keep your eyes wide open, girls. If he likes to pick fights with you and argue with you when you are dating, he will take that into the marriage. And that gets old very quickly! Ask yourself: "Would I rather have conflict or peace?" Advice from Mom: Observe how your date treats his mother, for the way a man treats his mother is the way he will treat his wife. Very smart advice.

God tells the older woman to encourage the younger woman to love her husband. It's the very first thing on God's list for the older woman to do, and it's not an easy task. But it has to be first. She is to love her husband first. The other six attributes are to fall in line behind loving him. The husband comes first, especially before the children. He will be—or should be—around after the kids have left, and when the honeymoon picks up again!

MOM SAYS

⤷ The Honeymoon Is Over

We don't "love" each other as we used to. The excitement is gone. It's down to the nitty gritty, and we both want out! We want to find a new love.

America is bombarded with sexual misinformation. Novels, TV, and magazines tell us of fictionalized romances that never die, and we believe them because we want to.

The Road Less Traveled by M. Scott Peck is a very good book on the realism of "falling in love." He says:

> We fall in love only when we are consciously or unconsciously sexually motivated. The second problem is that the experience of falling in love is invariably temporary. No matter whom we fall in love with, we sooner or later fall out of love if the relationship continues long enough. This is not to say that we invariably cease loving the person with whom we fell in love. But it is to say the feeling of ecstatic lovingness that characterizes the experience of falling in love always passes. The honeymoon always ends. The bloom of romance always fades.[14]

How to Cause Chaos

Let's look at two strong Christian authors and see what they have to say about marriage. In his book, *7 Ways to Wreck a Marriage*, J. J. Turner offers some important information about the marriages of today:

> The once-stable marriages that existed in our grandparents' day and in the days of their parents were only a fleeting note in the evolution of sociology. They have been washed away by a deluge in the tsunami of change.
>
> The traditional wedding vows of "for better or for worse": and "'til death parts us" are being abandoned, or at least given only lip service by many who take them at the marriage altar. One couple's

vows contained, "As long as we feel it is worth the effort." Every marriage, regardless of tenure, is subject to destruction by an unexpected tsunami.[15]

In Betty Bender's book, *What's a Woman to Do?* she wisely remarks:

LOVE is not as was acclaimed in the old movie, *Love Story,* "never having to say you're sorry." On the contrary, love is ever being ready and willing to say you're sorry.

LOVE is not calling your husband "pet names" in public—nor stroking him each time he comes close to you. I'm not being critical of such behavior, but more important is how you act toward him when the two of you are alone!

LOVE does not require continually having to be in his presence or always having to sit next to him when you are in the presence of others; as even in your separation you are fully committed to one another.

What can the older women teach the younger women about love? First of all, they will teach and demonstrate that love is an abiding commitment. It is pledging yourself to the other "for as long as you both shall live."

LOVE is learning to adjust to whatever may come in your life and to make the best of it, together.

LOVE is giving oneself to another without any reservation or holding back, wanting to make him happy and fulfilled in his life.

LOVE is always under control. It requires acting right even when you feel wrong. Love is not an emotion, although emotion grows from love. Love is the action. Emotion is the result of the action. In spite of what the world says, it is easier to act in our Christian way into the right feeling than to feel our way into the right action. The feelings will come with time if we continue to love as God showed us the way.

LOVE is more than "a many splendored thing." It is the essence of life as God wants us to live it.[16]

How Does God Feel about Divorce?

"For I hate divorce," says the Lord, the God of Israel, "and him who covers his garment with wrong," says the Lord of hosts. "So take heed to your spirit, that you do not deal treacherously" (Mal. 2:16).

Burton Coffman has this to say in his commentary on Malachi:

> God hates divorce. Our society loves divorce. The shameful acceptance of the wanton violation of the marriage covenant on the part of many today, to the extent of threatening even the holy institution of marriage itself, is a cruel, heartless, and brutal fact of our culture. We are rapidly drifting into a state of godlessness from which there might never be any complete return. It is a deadly cancer in our social order that should be of utmost concern to every thoughtful person. God's hatred of what many are doing ought to be a strong deterrent.[17]

The going rate right now on divorce statistics is that one marriage out of two ends in divorce. These statistics include the fact that many couples remarry the same spouse after divorcing them, but still the figures are mind boggling.

Too many give up on their marriage too quickly and feel there is no hope for salvaging it. Often the couple refuses to get counseling and the help that could change things. Many do not know where to turn. So feeling there is no solution, they file for a divorce.

Dr. J. J. Turner reminds us,

> The words "divorce granted" are pronounced all too often in the courts of the United States, as men and women blatantly disobey God's command: "Therefore what God has joined together, let no man separate" (Matt. 19:6). The divorce rate has declined in the past five years . . . One reason is that more and more couples are living together without the benefit of marriage . . .
>
> Divorce is the ultimate wrecking ball of marriage, a foe created by a husband and wife. It is a sign that marriage vows and promises have not been kept. It is a sign that love has not been extended beyond hurts and forgiveness. It is a sign that the attitude of Christ

was not practiced by both spouses. It is a sign that an easy solution was preferred instead of fighting to save the marriage.[18]

Satan, Sin, and Sex

You and I know about the Satan factor, right? He roams the earth looking for Christians to devour (1 Pet. 5:8). The world is full of Satan, sin, and sex. The world feeds on these things.

The workplace is rife with tawdry affairs. It is no longer uncommon to hear that a husband has left his wife for a man and a wife has left her husband for a woman.

Is this something new in the year 2021? Absolutely not. Solomon was inspired to write almost three thousand years ago that there was nothing new "under the sun." The ancient world was notorious for both homosexual and heterosexual adultery. Because of that base sexual sin, God destroyed Sodom and Gomorrah with fire and brimstone, never to be rebuilt.

When I read the account of the angels visiting Sodom (Gen. 19), I am always shocked at the behavior of the homosexuals pounding on Lot's door and demanding that the men (angels) come outside so that they (the city people) could have sex with them. How repulsive and disgusting.

And yet, it is just as disgusting for marriages to crash and burn because a wife fell for a man at her workplace. This coworker, she thought, was the opposite of her husband who snored, had bad breath, left his dirty socks on the bathroom sink, and scattered wet washcloths and towels all over the floor. A husband who didn't even have a clue about the meaning of the word "romance," and his only concept of "tender" was how he liked his steak.

Or perhaps a man left his wife for a woman at his office who listened when he talked, catered to his every need, made him feel "special" and dressed like a million bucks. His own wife who kept the home fires burning rarely wore makeup, hated sex, and was so busy running the kids here and there that she never cooked a single meal—the family only ate takeout.

It's Not Just the Kids or the Unbelievers

Folks, both of these scenarios have been lived out in front of most of us with the principal players being friends or relatives or even a brother or sister at church. Please don't let Satan fool you into believing Christians never sin or have affairs. Don't hide under that rock. And don't be fooled into thinking that only young people sleep around. It's simply not true.

People want to live their lives their way, so don't butt in! Don't cramp their style, and whatever you do, don't tell them anything God has to say. I recently heard about a retirement community in Florida that has the highest rate of sexually transmitted diseases in the state. Old folks are running around the community, having affairs—a sexual free-for-all, a "Woodstock for senior citizens!" You would think that these older folks would be prudent, acting like grownups should act, but they don't care what others think. There is no shame. It is disgusting to see this kind of behavior in those who should be examples of wisdom instead of lusting after one another. Talk about obscene!

If you live long enough, you will see Satan cleverly demolishing families in the church with all kinds of sinful problems. Some of these members are lost forever. I have seen congregations where affairs occurred in the family of God, and the hurt is real—on all sides.

Don't be afraid to admit you need professional help. Marriage counseling continues to save many a marriage. There is no perfect husband. There is no perfect wife. Every marriage needs work, so note the areas that are weak and go to work! Go to the Father in prayer. God is the Great Fixer, and He can fix anything. That is an absolute. Why? Because God loves marriages, and God hears prayers. Nothing is impossible with our Father!

A Sad State

Girls, when we are young we think we must have someone who is so wrong for us. Some women perilously put all their eggs in one basket, foolishly believing, "If I can just have so-and-so at the office. He is so exciting! He pays attention to me. He buys me little presents and is full of surprises. He is so sexy. I know that if he were my husband, I would be happy." This is how adulterous affairs start. Not once do they pray about it or consult God's Word. I cannot tell you how dangerous that kind of thinking is—and how sinful.

> You have heard that it was said, "You shall not commit adultery; but I say to you that everyone who looks at a woman with lust for her has already committed adultery with her in his heart" (Matt. 5:27–28).

Are we so naïve to think that Jesus' words are for men only? Of course not. Men do not own the market on lusting. When a woman looks at a man with lustful desires—whether or not either is married—she is committing adultery in her heart. And adultery is a definite sin. Jesus applied the principle of that seventh commandment to Christians. How easy it is for women to fool themselves into thinking that looking and lusting are fine for women but not for men.

Love 'em and Leave 'em

I have known of women who divorced their faithful husband, married that exciting lover, and lived to rue the day they walked out on that first marriage. They discovered that they only exchanged one set of problems with one husband for another set of problems with another husband! Many times the new husband has the very same irritating habits the first husband had, or even worse. These women soon discover that they have jumped from the frying pan right into the fire—again!

Many wish they could go back and reclaim that first husband, but it is often too late, for he has found someone else to love. Never, never,

never underestimate the power of Satan to reel any of us in by the lust of the flesh, the lust of the eyes, and the pride of life (1 John 2:16). Satan is an expert at wrecking our lives, and we can be so naïve.

›››› PAUSE AND PONDER ‹‹‹‹

Think back to the time you were very naïve in your marriage. Why should Christian women always be on guard to fight the temptation of "another man"?

A Personal Discovery

A group of my close friends and I once attended a ladies' retreat. We stayed at a nearby motel during the seminar and enjoyed late-night discussions, laughter, and food. As the weekend progressed, we laughingly talked about our families and children. Of course, we eventually discussed and compared our husband's antics, quirks, and peculiarities. By the time the weekend was over, each one of us couldn't wait to get back to our own home and husband! We had discovered that compared to others, our husbands were Prince Charming, Tom Selleck, and—as Goldilocks discovered—"just right." But God knew that all along.

Love, Love, Love

In 1969, Terry Garrity shocked the world with her book, *The Sensuous Woman*. Dubbed "the book that fired the first shot in the sexual revolution," Ms. Garrity opened the door for frank discussions of bedroom pleasures. (Anybody remember the Saran Wrap chapter?)

Yes, this is a very frank and sometimes explicit discussion, but we need to be honest about these things. Let's not be too shocked to discuss in the proper settings the sexual aspects of life. Too many times we are like Edith Bunker in the TV sitcom, *All in the Family*, who never could say the word "sex" but always spelled it, s-e-x, in any conversation.

My sweet sisters, love that man you married and satisfy him with your body and love! God has given him to you! Remember the things that made you fall in love with him. Do everything you can to keep the flame alive in your marriage! Surrender to your husband's love and need for you, and don't look back. And never forget that God invented the act of making love! God has so designed our bodies to need and want sex. He has graciously given the sex act to married couples to be used anytime they desire, not just for creating life. An active sex life is vital so that a couple's love will continue to grow and bind them to one another. It is in the act of surrendering oneself sexually to his or her spouse that deepens the soul of a marriage.

Read Patsy Loden's book, *Loving Your Husband*, which continues to be a best seller because it describes ways to keep marriages alive, sexy, and satisfying. (Be sure to read about Tarzan and Jane.) Isn't that what God wants for your marriage? Didn't God create the act of making love?

> When the Father presented Eve to Adam, she was naked, and they were not ashamed. When a husband and wife are in their own habitat, nakedness is not wrong; it is the way the Father planned life in Paradise. Did the Father want Adam to have full appreciation of the beauty of the wife? Yes, God made her especially for Adam's needs, which included sex. Both you and your husband should stand naked before one another in the flesh and spirit and become one as God commanded.[19]

What a marvelous day it was when God gave man and woman the gift of sexual love. Aren't you thankful?

Of course you are, and to prove that God approved of sexual love, He inspired Solomon to write a love manual over three thousand years ago. Yes, girls, long before Masters and Johnson there was the Song of Solomon. How amazing is that? God has thought of everything! And if you ask yourself why God would do this for us, just consider this: God loves you and me, and He wants us to have happy, fulfilled, glorious Christian marriages. How absolutely wonderful He truly is!

A Beautiful Love Song

Observe how Don McWhorter expressed "happiness" in his book, *God's Woman: Feminine or Feminist?*

> God's strategy for the happiness of mankind was the writing of a beautiful love song and the instrument He created to play that love song was the home—a man and woman living together after the ordinance of God in holy matrimony. Balance is the key to this divine arrangement. And gender is the key to the balance. God makes it clear that it is not in sameness of gender but in opposites of gender that this balance—and hence the beauty and function of the entire plan—is found. The sameness of unison might have seemed to some to be more equal and fairer but the resulting monotone would have destroyed the beautiful harmony God sought to achieve. It is in the blending of voices that are different, yet in the same key and the same song, that the beauty of God's strategy is seen. It is sad that the lilting melody is made a dirge by those who do not approve of, or appreciate, God's great mystery.[20]

Listen to the following practical and constructive advice from Mom.

MOM SAYS

What Does a Husband Need?

God says he needs to be respected. "The wife must see to it that she deeply respects her husband—obeying, praising, and honoring him" (LB). Another version: "and the woman must see to it that she pays her husband all respect" (Eph. 5:33 NEB).

He needs to know that the final say is his on differing opinions. She needs to know this, and the children must know it, too. He is the chief. He is the "house-binder." He is the one whose labor supports the family. He is the lifeline for food, clothing, sustenance, love, and direction.

Teach the children that he comes first. "Dad will be home soon. We need to clean up and look nice. Pick up your things because Dad likes for the house to look nice. He has worked hard, so don't go dumping on him your unhappiness."

Serve him first. Serve him his favorite piece of chicken. You are teaching your children to honor their parents. It used to be that the kids "took a cold tater and waited" until the adults were served. Now the papa is lucky if the neck is still on the plate by the time it gets to him. That's not right.

Send the children from the table if they cannot stop crying or yelling or whatever. This is prime time, and the children must be taught this. The world should not revolve around our children but our husbands. And already some mother is mad at me for such teaching.

The prayer is said. The father is served and then the children. Food is not piled on their plates to be thrown out after picked over. Put a little of everything on their plates, and no "I don't like" or "Yuk" is allowed. Teach them the food has been provided by God and is to be eaten with thanksgiving. With this process, the children in time will learn to like all foods. And parents will not have to endure constant tears and disturbances at the table. Mother teaches a lot of this before the meal. This is family time.

✒ WHAT DOES A MAN WANT IN A WIFE?

I was reading the result of a survey made asking this question, and they found that the men in these 1980s want the same thing men wanted in the 80s BC: simple compatibility, dependability, and a pleasing disposition.

Men want to come home to a sweet wife, a cheerful wife, a clean wife, and a happy wife. Her attitude is so important. Really, it sets the stage for the family. If Mama has a good sense of humor, there is a continual feast in the house. "All the days of the afflicted are bad, but a cheerful heart has a continual feast" (Prov. 15:15).

Washington Irving said it like this. "Honest good humor is the oil and wine of a merry meeting, and there is no jovial companionship equal to that where the jokes are rather small, and the laughter abundant."

Children seem to naturally have a good sense of humor. Have you ever noticed when you watch cartoons with them that you laugh at the same things? When our family gets together for a reunion, most of the time is spent retelling funny situations that happened in the past. And we tell the same things each time and laugh again.

The survey also found that "despite women's lib" the men polled didn't want their mates to be big bread winners—just loving companions. Men need to be loved and loved and loved. They may not even know they need it, but they do. We need to be touchers with our husbands and with our children. Touch often. Someone has to start the touching, and most times it is the wives. Babies can die without it and so can marriages.

Look Pretty!

Look as good as you can. Dress as well as possible. Learn to cover up what your figure lacks. Read magazines that help. Learn to pick the colors that look best on you, learn how to fix your hair, and learn what makeup is best. Be clean. Abby says a woman can't take too many baths. Use perfume that he likes.

Tell him how attractive you are. Don't ever point out your double chin or whatever. He might not have noticed it before. When you tell him, he will always notice it. I remember hearing a true story of a lady who always exchanged her husband's Christmas gift of lingerie. He always bought her something beautiful that was a size 12, and she exchanged it for a larger size with nothing said. If he thought she still wore a size 12, who was she to correct him?

Let him know often—do it every day!—that you admire his masculinity. Someone once said, "The two things that fracture the male ego most quickly are threats to his masculinity and fear of sexual inadequacy." He needs to know that he is an attractive man, and he needs to hear it from you most of all!

You married him by your own choice. You see an attraction others may not. I really feel that my husband is probably the most attractive man in the room! He knows I feel that way because I tell him. I tell him just by looking at him. I help dress him to look his best.

Touch him with non-sexual love and with sexual love. Kiss in the elevator, assuming that you two are alone. Always pick the table in the restaurant dining room that enables you to talk privately and cozily.

> *Your respect is his number one need.*

Always know where he is in a crowded room. Be looking for him as he looks for you, and let your eyes light up when you see him.

Write down ten things you like about your husband and thank God each day for those same things. Tell him often of his good points. Show your love for him in front of others. "Come and sit by me." Are you conscious of the women with happy marriages that you know? What do they think about your marriage?

Learn to be content in whatever state you are in: whatever house, whatever car, whatever clothes, whatever paycheck. He deserves praise for doing as well as he does. Your respect is his number one need. Don't forget that! Have sympathy for his role as provider for as long as you both shall live. Would you want that responsibility placed on you?

God did not make wives to be in competition with their husbands. Rather, after the fall, God said, "Your desire will be to your husband" or as one version says, "Your desire will be to please your husband" (Gen. 3:16). That is a gift from God to both of the marriage partners. God wants peace in the home. He tells the woman to please her husband, and he tells the husband not to be bitter against his wife.

Have you ever heard the story about the wife who went to her lawyer and said she wanted a divorce because she hated her husband?

She was only sorry that she could not think of something really bad to do to him before she left him for good. Her lawyer suggested a devious plan. He said, "Make him need you, and when you are gone, you can walk out laughing, and he will be crying."

So she did this. She became his slave—anything to please him. She worked at it, for she was a clever woman. Several months later she ran into the lawyer, and he asked if it was time to file the papers. And she said incredulously, "You think I'd leave that wonderful man?" She learned how to please her husband, and it resulted in him wanting to please her. They both fell in love again in the process. As she treated him as a king, he in turn realized he had a queen!

In Conclusion

Your husband needs you more than he needs any other person on earth. You are his woman, his mate, his other half, his friend, companion, lover. All that he lacked is in you. Find your niche in the circle of his arms. Hold onto him while you have him, for statistics say that you will outlive him ten years. The time will come when you wish you could pick up his dirty socks, or could find the toothpaste squeezed from the top, or could hear him driving in from work, or hear his voice calling on the phone, or find a card that you reminded him to buy that said "Happy Anniversary," or remember the Christmas Eves when he ran out at the last minute to get your present.

Hug him while you have him, for ten years is a long time to be alone.

True Love in Action

When you are married, you are positive that you are in love. However, true love comes years down the road, after the wedding, in the middle of financial troubles, kids, sorrows, and "test days." You see, it is in the toughest days that you truly see the hand of God working and doing and saving your marriage. There will be times that you will want to walk out the door, but you remember the vows you made before friends, family, and God. You decide to stay, and you are thankful you did. It is not the happy times that necessarily deepen our love, but it is the tough times that teach us what true love is. And there is a difference.

Trey and Lea Morgan from Childress, Texas, travel all across America teaching and helping Christian marriages with their Stronger Marriage Workshops. Trey once shared this on Facebook:

> My wife has brought me coffee today, told me that I was awesome, and fixed me supper. She loves me.
>
> I've let her sleep in, reminded her that she's beautiful, and filled her car up with gas. I love her.
>
> Marriage is about the little things. It's as good as two people are willing to make it. Marriage isn't always what you may think or hear; it's better.

The Best Piece of Advice

Here is a piece of motherly advice given by my own mom: "God can take any marriage and make it a success, as long as they both are faithful Christians." Note the key word here—*faithful,* which includes the gathering of the saints—that's a family reunion! Hebrews 10:25 tells us, "Not forsaking our own assembling together, as is the habit of some, but encouraging one another; and all the more as you see the day drawing near." Being faithful in attendance is a foundation for building great faith.

I think we forget that when we meet to worship our Lord that He is there, seeing us, watching us, and blessing us. God is an active participant in His family, loving His children and giving them the gifts, grace, and approval they need. And one of those gifts is spiritual growth.

⤛⤛⤛ **PAUSE AND PONDER** ⤜⤜⤜

What is the best piece of advice given to you before you married? How was it smart?

Let God Work

Have you ever noticed that when you are struggling with a certain problem, a preacher or teacher teaches a lesson on that very problem? I sure have. I believe that God provides all those precious lessons that you need for now and for tomorrow, and He sends them your way. His Word is powerful, and its scope is broad enough to address your every need. Let God work in your life! When your ears are open to His will, you will get just what you need at the time you need it. You can take that to the bank.

> It is in the toughest days that you truly see the hand of God working.

But if we are absenting ourselves from worship, we will miss out on the mighty life-changing lessons God wants us to hear, lessons that have the power to heal us, encourage us, and help us raise our families. God loves us that much! Don't keep God in a box, girls. Let Him out! We humans do not have the capabilities to imagine the power of God! See how magnificently He works in our lives through the power of His Word, not only to mature us as Christians, but also to equip us to help others, experiencing the same problems and challenges (2 Cor. 1:4; 5:17). That's just one of the many reasons it is important to stay faithful.

If you are not gathering with the family of God continually, year in and year out, for all the innumerable blessings worship and Bible study provide, you are going to miss out on everything! How does one describe the closeness of the family of God, the love that binds us together, and the daily walk with the Lord the church family inspires?

On top of all that, you will have lost the most precious thing a child of God can lose—Him! —not to mention your very soul! This is not how God intended any of us to live. Are we letting God work in our families? Or do we shut Him up with closed Bibles?

Here are some suggestions:

Be your husband's number one fan. Encourage him over and over to seek the Lord. Encourage him in his role of Christian, husband, and father. Encourage him to be the head of the family. That is the Lord's will for him.

Be your husband's personal cheerleader! Help him in his insecurities and inferiority complexes. Build him up.

Hold his hand! Hold hands during every prayer. It bonds you. It makes you forgive. It also softens your heart, especially if you walked into the church building madder than a wet hen. Remember, it is working on him too. Pray, pray, and pray some more for your husband. Pray for him to be the man God intends for him to be. Let God work on him, and let God work on you.

Get in the Word together! Read the Bible every day together. Read aloud for spiritual growth. It will increase your faith and you will talk more about the Bible as you walk through its pages. You will count your blessings as you see how magnificently the Lord has worked in your life together.

Make God happy! Serving God means serving your husband too. Be his everything. God is first, then your husband.[21]

God Knows Everything

You and I both know that. God is omniscient, omnipresent, and omnipotent. And this barely describes Him. It's just the hem of the garment when it comes to depicting the Almighty. The Father knows what your marriage needs, and He will give it to you. Surrender your marriage to Him. Listen to Him once again. He simply says first, "Love your husband."

Let's close this chapter by asking, "Am I prioritizing my husband?" Am I making him first in my life, after the Lord, of course?

Betty Bender, a precious mentor of mine, once held my hand in hers, looked me straight in the eye and said, "Take care of your husband. You have been placed here to support him and be there for him." I hope I never forget that.

Ronald Reagan once said, "There is no greater happiness for a man than approaching a door at the end of a day knowing someone on the other side of that door is waiting for the sound of his footsteps."

It is never too late to make adjustments, so girls, let's start now and do better. And above all things—let's please God! If God says to love our man first, then no questions asked—let's do it.

A WOMAN'S PRAYER

Oh, Father, I thank You for You. And I thank You for the blessing of a husband who loves me. Please, Lord, may we constantly tell You how much we love You for loving us and giving us the gift of the love a man and a woman can have in a marriage. How kind You are to let us experience this love! Thank You, sweet, sweet Father for looking into our hearts and seeing the needs there for this mate—the one You have chosen for us. May we always cherish one another, Lord, but above all, may we never stop cherishing You. In Jesus' name, Amen.

THOUGHT QUESTIONS

1. What is a husband's greatest need from a wife?
2. Name the two kinds of touching needed.
3. What can I do to keep or start communication?
4. What kind of love does a good marriage need?

♪ **Song: "Jesus Calls Us"**

Insights

Women Need Women

I must admit that my mom was incredibly intuitive. She was unusually sensitive to other people and could step back and look at most human situations/relationships and perceive quickly what was occurring—negative and positive. She knew how to "cut to the chase" when recognizing someone's character flaw—and cut quickly. She even had a knack for observing something and pointing out a hidden fact about you that you had never noticed. Enough beating around the bush. I am just trying to lay the foundation of how smart she was and how dumb I can be.

Years ago, our family attended a congregation of the Lord's people that offered quite a few challenges. Jeff and I were young and new to the area, so we had to find our niche. That was not easy.

As the years passed and our children were born, we found our comfort zone. Our preacher was an older man, very kind, but I did not consider him an interesting speaker. His lessons seemed very cut and dried, and I had trouble following him. I began to tune his sermons out. I found him boring, something I had frequently related to my mother.

Mom came to visit and attended worship with us. When the preacher got up to preach, Mom pulled out a piece of paper and took notes on his sermon, her habit for as long as I could remember.

After lunch when we had the kids put down for their naps, Mom beckoned me to sit with her on the couch. Together we started discussing the recent church service. She pulled her newly made notes out of her purse, and with a strong, compelling voice she taught the sermon again to me, point by point.

As she concluded, she looked directly at me while slowly putting her notes away and said, "That was one of the finest lessons that I have ever heard in my whole life." I was shocked, but I was even more shocked to realize that I had missed it—completely missed out on one of the finest lessons a Christian could hear.

How could I have missed such an opportunity to learn and to grow? What was I doing and what was I thinking? I had prejudged the preacher, the sermon, and even God by tuning myself out so completely. I had not given the preacher a second chance. God had sent a powerful life-changing message, and I had checked out mentally. As a result, I missed out on the sermon of a lifetime, all because I had not made the effort to listen to the wise teaching of an old preacher. Even if his approach was not particularly easy to follow, I neglected to write down the powerful scriptures from the mouth of God, and that was the least I could have done. The power of God's Word had been laid at my feet, and I had turned and walked away in my mind.

> *How could I have missed such an opportunity to learn and to grow?*

As I look back upon that incident, I ask myself how I could have been so foolish. I was young and immature, but God had much to teach me that day. I thank God for a mother who loved Him so much that she was unafraid to point out to her daughter the error of her ways, with a lot of love, of course. So much was at stake, and Mom realized it. If I had continued on this blind, deaf, and dumb spiritual journey, I would have missed out on much growth, wisdom, and knowledge from the Lord. And unwittingly, I would have led my children to do the same thing because children are always watching. I was a young mother who needed to learn a valuable lesson, and Mom unhesitatingly taught it to me.

Girls, so many times we think our opinions and perceptions are right, and they are not right. We think we have a handle on a situation or even a relationship, but we are as blind as a post. That can be very dangerous. Solomon warns us in Proverbs 14:12: "There is a way which seems right to a man, but its end is the way of death."

Sometimes we have to have an older woman—a mother or sister—take us under her wing and explain the way more clearly, even as Priscilla and Aquila did with Apollos in Acts 18 and as Naomi did with Ruth in the book of Ruth.

I am so thankful to the Lord for godly women who will step up to the plate and live Titus 2. This is not an easy passage for us women. So often we don't want to read it or hear about it, and we surely don't want the preacher to preach on it! So preachers don't preach on it. They know they would be roasted before they even got to the parking lot!

Don't we women fight Titus 2 when it ought to be the other way around? We need to love this passage! God's plan is for the older women to encourage the younger women. This takes guts! The tragedy is that most women don't want anybody telling them how to live their lives or manage their homes, not even God! Sometimes older women do not want to encourage and help the younger women.

> *The bridge that God desires to be built between sisters often stays broken.*

In many congregations, the older and younger women steer clear of one another. In the process they lose one of the most precious relationships a woman can have, the love of a Christian sister.

When my mom was dying, my heart was broken, and when she passed away, I thought I would die too. But there were older women in my life, my sisters, who loved me enough to wrap their arms around me and say, "Becky, I will be your mama now." Those were the words I wanted to hear and needed to hear. Since then I have gone to other women who were losing their moms, wrapped my arms around them, and told them I would be their mama too. This ministry of women goes on.

My desire is to help women. That is my ministry. I want to help my sisters who are my age and older. My heart goes out to them. But I also want to help my young sisters from teenagers to those married with children. My heart goes out to them too. You see, we are all the same at heart. Why oh why can't we bridge the gap between our ages and just love, love, love one another? Why do women hold one another at arm's length? Why are we hateful with each other? My sisters, this should not be the way it is.

As a result, the bridge that God desires to be built between sisters often stays broken and in disrepair. My precious sisters, God wrote these words in Titus 2 to women, and we cannot ignore them. God still rules, and the Scripture is still there in black and white, whether we like it or not. Just think of how much better the church and families would be if all the women therein laid their feelings at Jesus' feet, embraced one another, and just loved one another.

My mom took her role as a Christian mother very seriously. She was not afraid to rock her children's boats. And believe me, she rocked my boat many times! I think she always had a higher goal running through her mind, to save not only her household but whomever she encountered as well. Her goal was our souls.

I thank God for women like Lea Fowler. I also am forever indebted to the older women in my life who loved me, counseled me, and taught me the way more perfectly. I needed it that Sunday in Georgia a long time ago. Mom stepped up to the plate and hit it out of the ballpark. Thanks, Mom, for always being unafraid to say what had to be said so this girl could grow up right, "in the nurture and admonition of the Lord." It is the only way to live.

By the way, I never listen to any preacher or teacher now without taking notes. I learned my lesson!

CHAPTER 4

Love Those YOUNG'UNS

"... to love their children ..."

⇥ BABIES DON'T KEEP ⇤

Cleaning and scrubbing will wait till tomorrow,
But children grow up, as I've learned to my sorrow.
So quiet down, cobwebs. Dust, go to sleep.
I'm rocking my baby. Babies don't keep.

—Ruth Hulbert Hamilton[22]

Older woman, teach me to love what? My children? Seriously? Are you nuts? Of course I love my children—my precious kids! What mother doesn't love her own children? What is God thinking?

Don't think that failure to love your own child doesn't happen, sisters. It does. Stop and consider that some women abandon their babies in garbage cans to die, not to mention the mothers who abort their babies. According to the World Health Organization approximately 125,000 babies are aborted every day.[23] Tune in to any channel on television, and you will view accounts of children who are continually abused mentally, physically, and sexually. Stay tuned even longer and you will see the numbers of children who are exploited, slaves of sex trafficking, or even murdered. This tragic list goes on and on.

Burton Coffman once wrote about a parent's love:

At first glance it seems hardly necessary to speak of training one to love spouse or children; but as Ward noted: "Love does not always flow out of a person, even a wife and mother, as from a mountain spring. Love in the family requires thoughtfulness, and the mother has to work at it. Paul recognized this, and the older could inspire the younger."[24]

On the website of *Psychology Today*, Robert W. Firestone, Ph.D., explores the relationships of parents and their children:

Parental love enhances the well-being and development of children . . . In my observation of families, I have noted countless examples of well-meaning parents engaging in behavior that is insensitive, mis-attuned, or harmful to their children, while earnestly believing that they love them and have their best interests at heart. These parents are telling the truth, although on a defensive level, when they tell their adult children who have been emotionally hurt that they loved them and did the best they could for them. It's true: They did the best that they were capable of, but more often than not, they simply weren't able to really see their child as a separate person and meet his or her needs. No matter how well-intentioned, many people are unfortunately not prepared for the task of raising children.[25]

God knows His creation. He knows men, and He knows women. God simply says, "Older mamas, teach the young mamas to love their children." God knows what can go on in a woman's head and what she herself has experienced before becoming a parent. He knows how dysfunctional a family can be. He knows all the ins and outs of every single mother and father who has ever lived or will ever live, and His instructions will never be outdated. He is God. He doesn't have to go into detail.

MOM SAYS

∽ GOD MAKES SENSE

God teaches in an orderly way. First, He tells the older women to teach the younger women to love their husbands, for this relationship is the key relationship. The love for each other is the foundation of the new marriage. It takes three to make a Christian marriage: God, the husband, and the wife. It takes the same three to bring up Christian children and mold them into Christian adults.

Under the old law, God gave the honeymooners a year to get acquainted after the marriage vows were said. The man had the year off, a year to learn to know his wife, her needs, her wants, her strengths, and her weaknesses. A year to begin to lead and to feel responsible for his wife. A year for her to love to be the "held" and not the "head."

The wheel took the men away from their homes and into the factories. The computer helps to hold him there. It used to be that most men were around the house night and day. They were a part of birthing, living, and dying, and all that is in between. Divorce statistics teach us that was the better way.

∽ FATHERS, WHERE ARE YOU?

God said, "Fathers, do not provoke your children to anger, but bring them up in the discipline and instruction of the Lord" (Eph. 6:4 RSV). We tend to emphasize the first part of this verse and ignore the second part. "You [fathers] bring them up in the discipline and instruction of the Lord." Bring them up from the cradle to their wedding day with all of the discipline and instruction that they need.

God says, "Bring them up" and "Train up a child," and He gives explicit instructions on how to go about it.

> These words, which I am commanding you today, shall be on your heart. You shall teach them diligently to your sons and shall talk of them when you sit in your house and when you walk by the way and when you lie down and when you rise up. You shall

bind them as a sign on your hand and they shall be as frontals on your forehead. You shall write them on the doorposts of your house and on your gates (Deut. 6:6–9).

Talk to them four times: when you sit in the house, when you walk out of the house, when you lie down, and when you get up. That just about covers your waking hours and locations. Talk, talk, talk. Talk in season and out of season—when they want to hear it and when they don't.

Children are going to grow up—age wise—but that doesn't mean they were brought up. Children tend to listen to their fathers more— they take them more seriously than they do their mothers. Their voices are deeper; they are bigger and more impressive in appearance, and they tend to be sterner. Dads don't fool around and usually don't give the instructions as often as mamas do before they take action.

When will we ever learn that when God speaks it is not just for instruction, but it also is to tell us that this is the only way that things work? He just says, "Do it this way." It takes us a long time to learn that this is the only way.

"Fathers, do not exasperate your children, so that they will not lose heart" (Col. 3:21). This instruction is not given to mothers. Why? Because mothers put up with a lot more from the kids. We want peace quicker. We often get in the way of the father's discipline. This shows we are the weaker vessel. We "save" the child from deserved and needed chastenings. Don't we, mamas?

God says it this way:

You wives must learn to adapt yourselves to your husbands as you submit yourselves to the Lord, for the husband is the head the wife in the same way that Christ is the head of the church and the saviour of the body. The willing subjection of the church to Christ should be reproduced in the submission of wives to their husbands. The husband must give his wife the same sort of love that Christ gave to the church when he sacrificed himself for her. So men ought to give their wives the love they naturally have for their own bodies. The love a man gives his wife is the extending of his love for himself to enfold her . . . In practice what I have said amounts to this: let every one of you who is a husband love his wife as he loves himself, and the wife reverence her husband (Eph. 5:22–33 J. B. PHILLIPS).

Although God has taught us the correct way to run a Christian home, we realize that the ideal is still to be accomplished. We can work and pray for the ideal, but we can be comforted with the realization that God will help us raise our children in whatever circumstances we find ourselves. We learn to be a team. We start out knowing little or nothing about raising children, and our hearts' desire is to raise them into responsible worthy adults who bring glory to the name of Christ.

The Excitement

There is usually much ado and much excitement when a baby is anticipated to arrive in a family. It is a thrilling time for parents and the family. Typical activities include baby showers and the preparation of a "themed" nursery. Anticipation is high.

When our first baby was on the way, quite a few older couples commented to me in a laughing but half-serious tone, "Just wait. Enjoy the quiet now. Your life is getting ready to change . . . forever." I never did completely like the sound of that, but I quickly found that it was true.

Dad often said, "When you have a child, you have started something you will never finish." When you and I bring a child into this world, our DNA has manifested itself into another's body, and on and on it goes for generations. We cannot stop the continuation of our gene pool.

～※※～ MOM SAYS ～※※～

As we go through the valley of the shadow, the remembrance of the pain fades when we see that little face.

> Whenever a woman is in labor she has pain, because her hour has come; but when she gives birth to the child, she no longer remembers the anguish because of the joy that a child has been born into the world (John 16:21).

～ GOD SAYS A BABY IS A GIFT FROM HIM

> Behold children are a gift of the Lord. The fruit of the womb is a reward. Like arrows in the hand of a warrior, so are the children of one's youth. Blessed is the man whose quiver is full of them, they shall not be ashamed (Ps. 127:3–4).

God often gives children to women who are barren. "He makes the barren woman abide in the house as a joyful mother of children. Praise the Lord" (Ps. 113:9).

The bride who slept till noon now jumps up when the baby sneezes or coughs. When the baby cries, she thinks he is dying, and when he has stopped crying, she is afraid he's gone.

Much is being learned about babies that didn't used to be known. Babies know their mother's heartbeat and recognize her voice before birth. They need bonding and love and touching from day one, or they can die from lack of it.

The natural way was the home birth with all the family there, and many are going back to this. The natural way was breast-feeding, and we are learning now there are immunities from disease present. The most important part of nursing is that the two of you get to know each other. You have to sit down or lie down and rest and talk to each other. If you must bottle feed, still take this time to hold and get acquainted with your baby. How I wish an older woman had taught me this.

God expects the mother to do the holding, to be at home with her babies. Don't fall for this new psychology that the child will do just as well with a substitute. No matter how well a child seems to do with another, you will never know how much better they would have done with you. By the time we realize this, it will be too late, for they will be grown and gone. Young women naturally want to run, to be a part of the action outside of the home. Home gets boring; the excitement is in the marketplace.

Young women, honestly, don't you think it is odd when a young woman wants to keep house and watch babies? Isn't she a little weird, bovine, or dull?

∾ BE HOME WITH OUR CHILDREN

A child is only lent to us. They have it all to learn, and we are to be their favorite teachers, because we love them more than anyone else does or should. We willingly take on their responsibilities. We choose to sit up with them at night and take them to the doctor when they are ill. We have the awesome chore of shaping their minds and attuning them to God. We are responsible for their thought, actions, ideals, and character, and we cannot delegate this to anyone else nor should we want to.

I have seen young Christian women teaching their babies about God before they could talk. I have even seen babies whose first word was "God." What wise mothers!

Do we ask our children after their Bible classes what they learned? One time we asked our small son who he studied about that Sunday morning. He answered, "Adam McGeeve."

Everyday happenings give us many opportunities to point out the goodness or the discipline of God.

⇾⋙ MY MOTHER LOVED ME ⋘⇽

There never was a time that my mother didn't love
    me.
 She couldn't wait to see me when I woke up from my
    sleep.
She hastened to my side every time she heard me
    weep.
She ran through the house when she heard me at the
    door—
A smile on her face just to see me back once more.
She trained, tutored, taught me and didn't spare the
    rod.
She impressed me every day with a desire to please
    our God.
Her steps are moving slower but one thing I can see.
Through the years I've learned to love her
Just the way that she loved me.

                 —Lea Fowler

⸂ OLDER CHILDREN

The influence of home outweighs by far any other influence. Home
is headquarters. Home is where you talk to them when they get up
and when they walk with you and when they retire. You are their
greatest teacher!

I took my children with me from room to room and talked to
them when they were babies. When they were old enough, I put
them in a walker, and they followed me and talked to me. They're
grown now, but they still follow me from room to room! As they
grew older, when I cooked, they cooked too, and hung out clothes
with me and worked with me on whatever tasks had to be done.
We worked together, read together, napped together, and prayed
together.

You are developing a lifelong relationship, friendship, partnership, and loveship. You are learning to know and to love your child, and they are learning to know and love you.

Dr. Campbell says, "Most parents have a feeling of love toward their children and that they assume that the child knows it, but often he does not." He further says, "The greatest error today with parents is that they do not convey their great love to the child." Then Dr. Campbell explains that the reason they do not is because they do not know how. "So the children do not feel genuinely unconditionally loved and accepted. Because of this, everything is on a faulty foundation, and discipline, peer relationships, and school performance all suffer. Problems will result."

RAISING LEFTOVERS

How can we show them how much we love them when we are not with them? How can we give them ourselves when our prime time is given to others? Our children are getting "leftover" parents, and we are raising "leftover" children.

It really takes twenty-one years to bring up a child to be a young adult. I understand that the Jewish people used to say that a man is not a man until he is thirty, and there is a lot of truth in that. They can grow up without our constant care, but they will not be what they could have been without careful parenting from a parent who gives them quality and quantity time.

A Peanuts cartoon once said, "Happiness is hearing your mother's voice in the kitchen when you come home from school." When they come home from school is such an important time. There is so much to tell and fix and share. By the time parents come in at suppertime, the news is forgotten or put away because of harried parents with too many burdens of their own.

Most of us are familiar with the term "latch-key children." These are children who come home to an empty house with their own key. Over three million children between the ages of six and thirteen go home to an empty house. An estimated fifty thousand preschoolers are home alone.[26]

"A child left to himself brings shame to his mother" (Prov. 29:15 NKJV). Why not a father to shame? Because God knows that a father must work to feed his family, but that chore was not put on the mother. Child raising is often placed solely on the mothers, although God teaches that the fathers are to become more and more involved. Someone has to be with the children, and the punishment of Adam still must be paid daily by the man of the household.

WHERE DID ALL THE MOTHERS GO?

Some women have to work, and God knows and understands that. But often women are working for things. Drugs and liquor are at an all-time high, as well as abortion, pregnant teenagers, and suicides of teenagers. Where did all the mothers go?

"The latch-key child goes home and often hides. They hide in a shower or under the bed or in a closet or bathroom. They often turn up the TV at a loud volume and the parents never know because their children don't tell them." One girl said, "Because we don't want to worry her."[27]

It is critical for children and parents to have a close loving bond, and this will seldom be if the children are left to themselves. God pities the widows and the orphans, and how shall we answer when we make our children orphans?

I can hear the protests: "I have to work." "We could not live as we do without me working." That might be true, but can we live a little lower and trust God to see that we have enough? Are we giving to God as we are prospered? If we are, God is giving it back pressed down and running over.

Can't we find ways at home to help financially as the worthy woman did? God knows how to supply our needs. I worked part time when my children reached college age and can testify that it costs to work outside of the home. Many times it costs the second car with all its expenses, better clothes, a quicker more expensive way of cooking. It takes energy and planning and studying to know how to economize plus the desire to do so.

The woman, as God knows, does not have the physical stamina to work all day and then come home to do all she would have done if she had been at home. Hurry causes anger, and even children's needs can cause anger. The husband not taking the lead causes fresh daily anger, and the child often goes to bed feeling unloved and unwanted.

God doesn't tell us why to stay home and what the results will be when we don't. We know why often too late when the harm is done, and the twig is bent and the die is cast. This is one of the reasons that He instructs the older women to teach the younger women. "Don't let them lose their children," God says. You know when we lose our children, God usually loses them too.

Children reflect love; they do not start it. Our love or lack of it shows through them. Psychologists treating troubled children use a doll and watch a child play with the doll. Their actions show how they feel about their parents' love for them. Think about it! How would our children act with a doll to reflect our love and attention?

TOUCHING

Somewhere, somehow, someone is going to have to start this touching business. If our foundation in marriage is right, we are showing our love for each other, and the children are seeing it or the lack of it.

I've heard many people say that their families did not touch, and that is why they do not touch. Touching is absolutely imperative! Hug, touch, look with loving eyes at each other.

FORGIVENESS

Parents need to practice and teach forgiveness. God gives us a new day each day, and we don't have yesterday's strength. Don't hold grudges against your children. Don't hold their inborn temperaments against them. Forgive them for reminding you of your own imperfections or someone else's in the family. Don't punish a truly repentant child.

Teach them to be conscious of their own sins and to fix them with God and others. Teach them to know that the forgiven sin is at the bottom of the sea. Let them see you fix your sins and note your comfort because your sin is forgiven.

We used to have a little doghouse with five pegs on it and our names written on each of the pegs. When one of us offended another and would not fix it, his name was placed in the doghouse. The only way you could get it out was to repent and say, "I'm sorry." It was a healthy way of creating a good conscience. And our children got to see their parents repenting too.

God tells us to raise our children in the Lord. "Children, obey your parents in the Lord for this is right" (Eph. 6:1).

All sin must be repented of or punished. Our sins do find us out. God is not fooled. "Whatever a man sows that shall he reap" (Gal. 6:7). Fix the sin, and then refill the love tank.

∞ HOW ABOUT A ROD?

"The rod and reproof give wisdom" (Prov. 29:15 KJV). There's not much reproof that you can give a toddler, and there's not much need of a rod for a teenager. If we have been constant and totally involved as parents should be in the training of our children, reproof is about all they need as they grow older. It is only the fool's back that needs the stripes.

The one thing we must never permit with our children is defiance or rebellion. This is an attitude of having to have one's own way. It is a meeting of wills and a determination to win at any cost. These occasions arise with every child because "foolishness is bound in the heart of the child and the rod of correction will drive it far from him" (Prov. 22:15 NKJV).

If we have been the loving parents we should be, the child will hurriedly seek to restore the loving relationship. A rebellious child is at war, and he has to know that he is not going to win the war.

Pity the child who does win. There is a principle here, a principle of obedience and authority. "Correct your son, and he will give you comfort; he also will delight your soul" (Prov. 29:17).

If we are having too many battles, then we need to see what we are doing wrong. Maybe we are overly strict and unrealistic with our children, and our desires for them are unrealistic too. We have to continually pray for wisdom. God knows how to raise children, and we don't!

A child soon learns if we are being fair or unfair. They soon learn when we really want them to mind and when it is important to us. They continue to test us to see where the boundaries are. Many parents do not know that children need boundaries for security.

We are trying to teach them how to be good parents. The oldest child is usually a different child. Either we were too strict or too lenient. We gradually change—hopefully for the better. We learn that a fault is not necessarily a permanent part of his character.

Haven't you often heard the question, how can one child turn out badly when all the others did well, and they had the same parents? No, they really didn't have the same parents. We are learning and changing, and we tend to change our methods as we grow older. It is usually conceded that the very young or the very old should not raise children. We tend to be too strict when we are very young and too permissive when we are very old.

After the rod has been applied to the posterior and the tears are flowing, sobs and snuffling are in evidence, then what? Campbell advises, "Give them time to cry awhile and think awhile, but stay near to pick up the pieces and refill the love tank." It is a mistake to start loving them immediately. This is confusing to them. They should have been warned what the consequences would be if they disobeyed and then told again during the make-up session. They need to be reassured that you still love them though they themselves probably wonder why! Reassure them that there is nothing they can do that will stop your love. Then remind them that love requires you to enforce the rules.

How many times have you heard people say that the Bible says, "Spare the rod and spoil the child"? It does not say that, rather it says, "He who spares his rod hates his son" (Prov. 13:24 NKJV). Some love their children so much that they cannot spank them; others love theirs so much, they can.

When your child is still rebellious after the spanking, you stopped too soon. They will rush to be loved when the chastisement is right. The love tank needs to be refilled, and they know it.

Here is another essential point: Parents are always responsible for their children wherever they are. We have all had children visit our homes who apparently belonged to no one. They were allowed to jump on the beds, hit other children, and fall on the floor in hysterics. No one moves. The hostess does not dare; the other mothers don't know what to do, and the child is free to terrorize. Usually the mother does not want this child to be corrected. Perhaps she feels she is on neutral ground, and the child gets in free. I have even heard parents say after they are struck by their own child. "He feels he has me over a barrel because we are around company." Who gave him that feeling?

It seems unbelievable that you have to tell many parents that they are not to allow themselves or others to be hit by their own children. Some even laugh at it and think it cute. But it won't be that funny when your child is old enough to injure another, even the parents themselves. You are to be in control of your child. If he is not your responsibility, whose is he?

Have you ever noticed the emotional stability of such a little tyrant's mother? She is frazzled and harried. She knows the child is out of control, and she feels almost immobilized by the child's forceful behavior. Somehow she lost the upper hand, but God says that not only can she regain control, but she can also have peace again in the home—and in other people's homes. Again, look at

Proverbs 29:17: "Correct your son, and he will give you comfort; he will delight your soul."

⚭ Pre-Teaching

I have found a lot of help in "pre-teaching." For instance, you might say, "We are going into the Smith's house, and you are not going to jump on the bed, hit others, or throw fits. If you do, I will do such and such." And then you do that. Never let your child intimidate you. It isn't right, and he knows it isn't right. He will lose respect for you if you continue in this sort of non-action. You can go into a private room, a car, or just go home and do the discipline, but do it for everybody's sake. A well-disciplined child notes the undisciplined with disapproval.

A tyrannical child is unloved by others, and how can we let our child be an unloved child? The rod, reproof, and love are our answers.

After the confrontation, remember there needs to be a lot of love—not indulgence but love—sharing, laughing, praising when you can. As Dale Carnegie says, "Be hearty in your approbation and lavish in your praise." Every human needs it. "It is by his deeds that a lad distinguishes himself if his conduct is pure and right" (Prov. 20:11).

It is difficult to endure sound teaching—especially to mothers about their children. We are emotional tigers about our children.

Hebrews 12:9–10 states, "Furthermore, we had earthly fathers to discipline us, and we respected them . . . for they disciplined us for a short time as seemed best to them." Often we, as their children, benefited or suffered or both. This causes us to be on the defensive and to answer quickly when reprimanded: "You raise yours your way, and I'll raise mine my way."

What is God after with us? What is He trying to produce in us, His children? Holiness, righteous living, happiness here and eternal life with Him. So He continues to discipline us daily. "And reproofs for discipline are the way of life" (Prov. 6:23).

We discipline our children for "a short time." God knows just how short it is before they are gone. God knows if we aren't rightly raising our children, then we are wrongly raising them. If we are wrong, they will never be holy, righteous, happy here or with Him in eternity. He tries to get our attention, and one way is through older Christian women. Can we love our children enough to lovingly listen to you, older woman? Can we love our children enough to listen to you, Holy Father?

Becky, Walk the Walk

It certainly is true that if we do not teach our children to love Jesus, the world will teach them not to. If our goal is to give our children the very best the world has to offer in schools, fashion, sports, and entertainment, then we might as well kiss our children's souls goodbye. However, if we have decided to bring our children up in the "nurture and the admonition of the Lord," our work begins when our babies are in the womb—telling them about Jesus who died for them. It means singing to them and praying for them constantly. It means being a godly example and being faithful in attendance. It means walking the walk ourselves. It means making the decision to do everything possible to get the whole family to heaven.

Going to heaven will be no accident. Heaven is a prepared place for a prepared people, and it takes work on our part. What a tragedy if we parents blissfully ignore God's rules and regulations and leave the child to his own "making." If we choose to ignore God and focus on surrounding our children with the world, the bottom line is that we really do not love our children. We love Satan more. It takes a whole lotta love, a whole lotta discipline, and a whole lotta talking about the Lord to help our children get to heaven. It takes two parents, if possible, who love and obey God and His Word *first* before a child can be brought up in the "nurture and the admonition of the Lord" (Eph. 6:4 KJV).

A WOMAN'S PRAYER

Our Holy Father, we praise Your name again and again for this life You have given us to give. Thank You, O Lord, for Your love in sending our brother Jesus to die on Calvary for each one of us. We can never do or be enough to earn this great gift. So, Father, help us to always love one another. Help us to tell one another how much we love each other. Help us to be bold in our love for You and for our children that You have given us. Bless our homes, God. Help us to lead our children home to You. In Jesus' name, Amen.

THOUGHT QUESTIONS

1. How are Christian women often influenced by the examples of worldly women?
2. Is it a temptation to leave our responsibilities? Support your answer.
3. What if our "responsibilities" were taken away from us?
4. Why is it necessary to discipline a child? Discuss methods of discipline.

♪ **Song:** "Seek Ye First"

Insights

It's All Going to Burn!

Have you ever contemplated the world around you: the sunsets, the sunrises, the trees, the sky, the ocean? How do you describe the beauty of God's paintbrush? What words do you use? Breathtaking doesn't even begin to describe His gifts for our pleasure.

When our little family moved to New England to do mission work, it was as if a huge light bulb suddenly turned on. Before our eyes lay God's works of art in mountains, trees, oceans, and lakes. Artists try to capture its splendor, but it really is impossible to "paint" New England—especially in the fall. I believe autumn in New England is truly the eighth wonder of the world. That must be what all the "leaf peepers" feel as they make their annual trek to New England.

Living there is like living in a postcard—scenes that should be shared with the world surround your daily trips to the grocery store or to the church building or just walking down the lane. You feel like you are living right smack dab in the middle of a Currier and Ives painting. These scenes not only take your breath away but also make you gasp. That's God at work!

Now that I have your attention, let me tell you about the uique people. They are tolerant, observant, frank, and generous. But most of all they make the most wonderful Christians. In my mind, the New Englander comes to Christ with the attitude: "It's all or nothing at all." The Christian from New England is "all in."

Friends, family, and brethren would question my parents' reason for leaving Oklahoma and Texas for the Northeast. They didn't quite understand the hearts of my missionary parents. My mom would turn to whoever had asked why we were departing and say, "Because the people are so worth saving."

Mom and Dad and their three kiddos—Tom, Judy, and Becky—embarked on an adventure of a lifetime in 1957. New England became our home, and we thrived there. We instantly loved the snow—I still miss it—and all the seasons. Something happens to you when you visit New England, and something even bigger happens when you move there. It seems to become a part of your DNA. It becomes home, and it will be home to you no matter where you live, as long as you live.

I could write all day about the fabulous food and how the song "Autumn Leaves" made us cry when we left New England. But I must tell you about one delightful aspect: the antiques. There's nothing more beautiful than an old barn by the side of the road, chock full of furniture, spinning wheels, quilts, and dishes, boasting the sign: BARN SALE TODAY!

The New Englander comes to Christ with the attitude: "It's all or nothing at all."

Mom and Dad adored the antiques, the stores, the barns, the store-owners—everything about "antiquing," as Mom called it. It was an education in history. Mom had this theory that if you visited any of these sights on a regular basis, eventually something would grab your eye, be it old desks, wicker furniture, Blue Willow dishes, cut glass, or whatever. You would develop an interest, and soon you would be addicted like everybody else in New England.

Well, there were quite a few things that grabbed Mom's eyes, most of them being rose dishes. Rose plates, rose bowls, and the item that we all soon adored: The chocolate pot. Chocolate pots became a delight to Mom, and she found quite a few at auctions, garage sales, and barns.

Porcelain chocolate pots arrived on the American scene in the late 1800s during the Victorian Era. They are beautiful but breakable pots with snub spouts, similar to a coffee pot and often hand painted. But the chocolate pot is much more delicate, often having small, matching cups and saucers. These lovely pots held hot chocolate to be served sparingly with tea cakes, cookies, and other treats.

She knew that he was the most valuable possession in the room.

Chocolate was a delicacy in the Victorian Era. The pots are very exquisite and can be ornate, fancy and beautifully painted. Naturally the ones with roses were the most beautiful, according to Mom.

Somewhere along the line, Mom bought a lovely mahogany whatnot stand. The six-foot beauty had fancy lines with ornate shelves that graduated from small to large. Curved legs supported it and, of course, it was perfect for displaying Mom's chocolate pots.

Years went by. I left home, married, and had two precious children, Jennifer and Jeffrey. We lived outside Atlanta and were able to visit Mom and Dad in Maine fairly regularly because Jeff worked for Delta Airlines. It was on one of these visits that the "Chocolate Pot Story" occurred.

Two-year-old Jeffrey was in front of the whatnot stand at the bottom of the stairs perusing the whatnot shelves and pots. Mom and Jeff were nearby. I was midway down the stairs when the next few moments immediately turned into "slow motion mode" as I saw my two-year-old begin to climb the whatnot stand. Well, it did kinda look like a fancy ladder. As he took his first step on the bottom shelf, the whole piece of furniture started to topple. I noticed the chocolate pot on the top shelf hit the chocolate pot on the next shelf which in turn hit the chocolate pot on the next shelf, until all five shelves with five Victorian chocolate pots landed on the floor, along with the overturned whatnot stand. I was living a chocolate pot nightmare.

I remember hollering, "Jeffrey," grabbing him, and swatting him. Mom quickly turned and left the room. Jeff started picking all the remains up and straightening the stand back up where it belonged. I was so upset and so horrified that it was "my child" who caused this disaster.

Mom walked back into the room about five minutes later and came to my side. "Becky, it's okay. First of all, these chocolate pots are just "things." They are going to burn someday. Second, your sweet Jeff is a new Christian. I must set the right example for him. What would he think of me, his mother-in-law, if I got bent out of shape over "things"? And third, if anybody—anybody—is going to break my chocolate pots, I sure am glad that it is my grandson!"

Jeff, Mom, and I picked up the chocolate pots and pieces and took them into the kitchen where we could see if any were salvageable. As it turned out, only one chocolate pot lost its life (the top shelf one), and one chocolate pot had a huge chunk taken out of it. (Mom promptly stuck an ivy plant in it, and no one noticed.) But for all practical purposes, the rest survived.

For me, the young wife and mother who was watching this scene play out, I realized it was Mom who got the Oscar. She kept herself together. She didn't lose it, no matter how valuable the broken possession might have been to her. She knew what was most important—her example to her son-in-law, the new Christian. She knew that he was the most valuable possession in the room. (She also was very happy that the loss was minimal, and she still had other chocolate pots left.)

There are always lessons to be learned and remembered when disaster strikes a home, and this was no exception. Mom had always tried to impress on us children that things were only things, and one cannot serve two masters (Matt. 6:24). On this particular day, she was put to the test. Mom had to practice what she preached.

Mom continually taught us and others the paraphrase of 2 Peter 3:10: "Never get caught up with material possessions, because they will burn up along with the earth at the second coming of Jesus."

The chocolate pot lesson was a Titus 2 lesson, for it reminded me to be sensible about worldly things. It offered a time for all of us to re-evaluate our priorities, and I always knew where Mom stood on that! God was number one with Lea Fowler and would always be in her life. She loved God so much that she lived for God. If a grandson climbing her whatnot shelf threw a wrench in her faith, she quickly recovered and was back on track in a matter of minutes. I am sure Mom's faith was very frustrating for Satan, and I hope it drove him nuts.

Girls, I am so grateful to this woman for loving me and having the courage—and guts—to live out her faith in front of all who met her. And then she had the gumption to wrap her arms around the daughters of the King and teach them how to live out their faith for the Lord too. She certainly took to heart "older women teach the younger women." No wonder so many called Lea Fowler "Mama"! We can certainly imitate that, my sisters, so why don't we?

Now you have the insight from the antique-disaster-tale that taught our family. But what I love most is what happened many years later. In the last years of her life, Mom had me write down what to give to my siblings and the grandchildren when she died. One day she looked at me and said with a little chuckle, "Beck, give the whatnot stand to Jeffrey. I want him to have it."

Whatnot shelf with chocolate pots and cups

CHAPTER 5

Act Like You Got Some SENSE!

"... to be sensible ..."

When I was a young kiddo playing with my friends, we sometimes said to one another, "You are so stupid!" We didn't think a thing about it. When I became a young mother, I noticed that suddenly the word "stupid" was a definite no-no, as well as the word "dummy." I blame it on *Sesame Street.* Also in the South, some mamas are known to holler these words at their children: "Act like you got some sense!"

Yes, words like "stupid" and "dummy" are deemed as unfit language. They are offensive, able to hurt people's feelings, and can wreak havoc on one's ego and self-esteem. I will not deny that. However, sometimes these words can be used by God to describe a situation He wants us to beware. God can use any word He wants, and we humans need to hear it. We know that 2 Timothy 3:16 teaches: "All Scripture is inspired by God," and we believe it. God's words given to us in the Bible are breathed from His lips. If God wants to use the word "stupid" or "dummy" or "fool," He has that right—He invented words.

Note these few times in the Bible that one of these words is used (NASB):

- ✣ Psalm 49:10—"For he sees that even wise men die; the stupid and the senseless alike perish and leave their wealth to others."
- ✣ Psalm 92:6—"A senseless man has no knowledge, nor does a stupid man understand this."
- ✣ Psalm 94:8—"Pay heed, you senseless among the people; and when will you understand, stupid ones?"
- ✣ Proverbs 12:1—"Whoever loves discipline loves knowledge, but he who hates reproof is stupid."
- ✣ Jeremiah 10:21—"For the shepherds have become stupid and have not sought the Lord; therefore they have not prospered, and all their flock is scattered."

God Is Blunt

Somewhere along life's way, my mom discovered a version—sorry, I cannot find it—that translated Proverbs 1:22 that Wisdom had called out to people and said, "How long will you love being stupid?" I have found a translation that says it this way: "How much longer will you enjoy being stupid fools?" (CEV).

Pretty blunt, don't you think? What's the point of all these "foolish" and "stupid" words? It is very simple. God does not want His children to be stupid. Period. He doesn't want us to act like idiots when it comes to behavior or obtaining knowledge. God wants us to use the brains He has given us and to act sensibly.

Is It Wrong to Say "Fool"?

Many times when I had a problem understanding the definition of a word, Mother would say, "Well, let's just think about that word for a minute. What is the opposite of it?" Together we would explore antonyms and synonyms. This works! It's a great way to define and understand a meaning and concept. By the way, it's great training for playing the game Password too.

The book of Proverbs spends a lot of time on the concept of a fool's behavior. We are very careful with that word *fool,* aren't we? I was told all my life, growing up, never to call someone a fool because Jesus said not to do that. Let's examine His words.

> But I say to you that everyone who is angry with his brother shall be guilty before the court; and whoever says to his brother, "You good-for-nothing," shall be guilty before the supreme court; and whoever says, "You fool," shall be guilty enough to go into the fiery hell (Matt. 5:22).

Burton Coffman had this to say about "you good-for-nothing" and "you fool":

> The expressions are essentially the same, and the plain teaching of our Lord in this context is that *all* insults of every kind are sinful and that all our derogatory and deprecatory expressions against one's fellow human beings are murderous. Those who resort to the use of such expressions are guilty in the eyes of the Lord. This is true because such expressions find their origin in a heart full of hatred and enmity.[28]

One Who Is Not Sensible

Let's define what a fool really is: a person who acts unwisely or imprudently; a silly person, an unwise person. One of the definitions that I like the most is this: a fool is not someone who can't learn but one who refuses to learn. That is a great definition.

Many times, acting like a fool can be a choice. One who is foolish and insensible has surely chosen that path for one reason or another. Perhaps it's to weasel out of working or being held responsible or being held accountable. It is easier to act like a foolish child, claim ignorance and naivete, and escape all kinds of wrath and punishment because others will make excuses for you. Perhaps a person does not mind looking foolish. Sometimes, as a result, that person starts to believe the falsehood, that she is incapable and unintelligent.

With God's Help, Come to Your Senses

What is the definition of *sensible?* Having or using good sense or sound judgment, cognizant, keenly aware. What is the opposite of *sensible?* Insensible. What are synonyms of *insensible?* Asleep. Numb. Unaware. Incognizant.

Some translations have the words *sober-minded* for the word *sensible.* What is sober-minded? Here are a few definitions according to some commentary writers:

- ❖ Prudent, in control of self.[29]

- ❖ Sober-minded . . . this quality is actually to be manifested by all Christians. It means having all faculties under control, well-balanced, even tempered, and realizing the importance and seriousness of life.[30]

- ❖ Calm and collected in spirit, temperate, dispassionate.[31]

We must always remember the sign that says: God doesn't make any junk! And He doesn't, girls. He has given all of us brains and talents. There is something we can do for the Lord—even if we are a one-talent woman. Read the parable of the talents in Matthew 25:14–30. Remember, the impossible is possible with God (Matt. 19:26), and any fool can change with God's help.

Do you remember that wonderful parable Jesus told of the prodigal son in Luke 15? The younger son demanded his inheritance prematurely—before his father had even died! How rude and insensitive this young man was. The loving father gave both sons their inheritances, and the younger set out determinedly on his path of sensuousness and self-destruction.

We all know the story of how the young boy soon found himself friendless and employed with the task of feeding pigs. How far this Jewish boy had sunk in his short life. Not from rags to riches, but from riches to rags. Did he accept his circumstances?

> But when he came to his senses, he said, "How many of my father's hired men have more than enough bread, but I am dying here with hunger!" (Luke 15:17).

Note the beginning phrase of this verse: "But when he came to his senses." Up to this point he had been stupid, a fool, and insensible. He suddenly realized what he had done; he made a decision to change his life; he came to his senses.

⟫⟫ PAUSE AND PONDER ⟪⟪

Explore 1 Samuel 22:13–15. Why did David act so crazily? Now think of opposite behavior: serenity. Research the popular poem, "Serenity Prayer" and discuss how it is also "sensible."

On a lighter note, someone cleverly and humorously rephrased that poem with these words: "Grant me the serenity to accept the people I cannot change, the courage to change direction when I see them coming, and the wisdom to not try to smack some sense into them when I can't avoid them."

The Wise Woman

God is so kind to freely offer the incredible gift of wisdom to all who ask Him: "But if any of you lacks wisdom, let him ask of God, who gives to all generously and without reproach, and it will be given to him" (James 1:5).

Note how kind God is as He gives us this wisdom. He gives it to us "without reproach." What does that mean? He gives us wisdom without scolding us, without chiding us or saying, "Well, what took you so long?" He mercifully helps us in our pursuit of it. We don't wake up one morning with our heads full of knowledge and wisdom popping out of our ears.

As we study and read God's precious words, we see godly wisdom at work. He helps us to comprehend His righteousness as we study. When we view the good, the bad, and the ugly circumstances in which His people were involved, we see His loving hand working things out for those He loves. Will He not do the very same for us?

> And we know that God causes all things to work together for good to those who love God, to those who are called according to His purpose (Rom. 8:28).

The first three words of this passage are: "And we know . . . " My question is: Do we *know*? Do we know that God will work our problems out for us? Do we know this scripture because it is written on our heart? Do we know because it is memorized in our brains? Do we know God's Word at all? How does Romans 8:28 help us in our search for wisdom?

The Pattern of Proverbs 31

Using wisdom is being sensible. God so cleverly illustrates for us how wisdom is necessary in this life, and wisdom from God offers salvation. How important it is to invite Lady Wisdom into our lives and let her dwell there!

PAUSE AND PONDER

Take time to read the famous passage on Lady Wisdom from Proverbs 1:20–33 and use your Bible to glean more understanding:

1. Circle the questions asked by Wisdom.
2. What happened when Wisdom called?
3. What response was given to Wisdom's counsel and reproof?
4. Why should we listen to Wisdom?

What Does God Want?

But what does God want His children to be? He wants us to be in our right minds with our eyes wide open! He wants us awake, aware, and cognizant of the world around us. Of the church and all its needs. Of being in God's Word and handling it correctly (2 Tim. 2:15) in order to help others who are lost. He wants His daughters to be sensible in their homes where they lead and guide. My preacher friend, Frank Chesser, calls us "the queen of the home." Homes that are dedicated to the gospel call. Homes that are organized so that loving and learning can occur. Homes where husbands are cherished and children are loved and disciplined. In other words, my sisters, God does not want us women to be foolish, senseless, and heedless of what is going on right under our own roofs! He desires us to be wise, realistic women.

Keep your eyes wide open to the antics of children and teenagers. I always knew to check on my kids when the house got really quiet. That usually meant they were up to no good and were probably involved in mischief of some sort—matches, poison, anything lethal!

⟫⟫ PAUSE AND PONDER ⟪⟪

Examine 2 Timothy 3:1–6 in light of being a "Titus 2 woman." What action is commanded toward "such people" in verse 5? Focus especially on verse 6. Look up at least three translations of the word used to describe the women who were taken captive. How does this teach you to be a wise woman?

Do You Know Where Your Children Are?

Always know where your children are, my sisters, what they are doing, and who they are with. Always be smart; have a curfew and abide by it. Enforce rules and enact the consequences if your child disobeys.

Parents make a huge mistake when they allow a teenage child to go into her bedroom with a friend of the opposite sex and close the door.

Perhaps the child will say, "Oh, we are just going to do our homework or watch TV—or whatever." But Satan himself closes that door and hands over to your teen a key that opens Pandora's box with a loaded gun inside. Keep your eyes open, and don't be the mom who gives the kids an opportunity to sin. While you are doing all you can to keep your precious children pure, Satan is showing them how beautiful the gates of "Sheol" are!

Don't be naïve about kids and sex. You were young once, and yes, you do remember! Didn't Satan tempt you too? You may not be aware of what your child knows or has already done. Be wise, and don't let Satan use you to get to your child. In that bedroom is a bed and sexy music. Enough said. I don't have to draw you a picture.

My parents allowed a boyfriend to stand at the threshold of my bedroom and view my bedroom, and that was it. No boys allowed in my or my sister's rooms—none. Never. My husband, who was not raised in the church, has often told me that his parents told him that his bedroom was off limits to any girlfriend. That nips any home hanky-panky in the bud. I know of a sweet, single, young professional lady who dictates that no young man is allowed to step foot into her apartment. Period. Goodbyes are said at the door, so there are no worries of desires getting out of hand.

What can a parent do with teenagers who entertain friends in the house? Just say no to the bedroom and its obvious attractions and offer snacks and study time at the dining room table. Kids love food! But be aware; kids are very smart. Learn to outsmart them! They may schedule a "rendezvous" at someone else's house where there is no adult. You must be on your toes when it comes to kids who suddenly appear in your home. Know where your precious children are at all times, and know their friends.

Sweet Mama, wherever you are, I say this with all the love in my heart: Be sensible. Don't leave two sex-charged teenagers alone in your house, and whatever you do, don't let them close that door unless they're married. We've heard many reports of a young girl getting pregnant in her own bedroom or in the basement recreation room. Be wise, my sisters. God warns all parents when He says, "The rod and rebuke give wisdom, but a child left to himself brings shame to his mother" (Prov. 29:15 NKJV). How interesting this proverb ends with "mother." In this situation doesn't the father feel ashamed too? Yes, the father does, but the shame is felt more deeply by the mother, keeper of the home.

Don't fool yourself into thinking your daughter can deal with certain temptations just because you could at her age. Your daughter is not you! Many a parent has put too much trust in her child, and unwittingly has contributed to that child's downfall. Often, too much temptation engulfs the youth and she cannot handle it. When you are unwise, unaware, naïve, and senseless, it can result in more than one ruined life. Be smart and wise, and remember, Satan will always do anything to help your child sin. He invented it.

PAUSE AND PONDER

Discuss the rules you had at your home when you were young. List at least four wise guidelines for teens.

MOM SAYS

To Be Sensible

"How long will you love being simple?" Or "How long, O naive ones, will you love being simple-minded? And scoffers delight themselves in scoffing, and fools hate knowledge?" (Prov. 1:22).

When are we going to grow up and learn that naivete is childlikeness, and maturity is to be desired? We can't help being young, but with God's daily wisdom, we can leave immaturity and exchange it for happiness and reality. In time.

> We are no longer to be children, tossed here and there by waves, and carried about by every wind of doctrine, by the trickery of men, by craftiness in deceitful scheming (Eph. 4:14).

We are not to be kids any longer, for if we are, we will be quickly deceived. Satan's favorite tool is deceit. Eve was deceived; she was naive; she was fooled. We don't have an example of her being fooled the second time. Her price of naivete was too great and long lasting. The gates of Eden were forever closed.

It takes time and practice to learn what God says about everything. We can in a good conscience do many things as a new Christian that, in time, we have to put away.

> For though by this time you ought to be teachers, you have need again for someone to teach you the elementary principles of the oracles of God, and you have come to need milk and not solid food . . . But solid food is for the mature, who because of practice have their senses trained to discern good and evil (Heb. 5:12–14).

These people had gone backwards. They had once been teachers, but now they needed the ABCs again. We too are growing, or we are slipping back. We use it or lose it. If we are not daily in the Word and praying for wisdom in our lives, then we are regressing instead of progressing. It is only by practice that we can train our senses to know what is good and what is evil in the sight of God.

The next verse, Ephesians 4:15, says, "But speaking the truth in love, we are to grow up in all aspects into Him, who is the head, even Christ." We are to grow up and no longer want to be a child.

Why would you want to be a child? Because it is hard to be an adult. The buck stops with you instead of the indulgence you once felt. I remember when I went to college. What a shock! My teachers before had always wanted me to pass and encouraged me. To fail would have been just about as hard on them as on me!

I went to a state school during the depression. There were seven male students to every female. The teachers did not want any children; rather, they insisted that you be an adult. They called you by "Miss" and "Mr." They assured you that they graded on the curve which means that there would be some who would fail no matter what the grades. They encouraged you to quit if you were not serious about learning. You could attend class or not, keep notes or not, fail or pass. It meant nothing to them, whatever your choice. You really got the message that they hoped you chose to fail so they could be rid of you and then would deal only with the committed.

You know, if you think about it, God gives this same sort of logic when He says,

> I know your deeds, that you are neither cold nor hot; I would that you were cold or hot. So because you are lukewarm, and neither hot nor cold, I will spit you out of my mouth (Rev. 3:15–16).

Which is another way of saying, "Grow up or else!"

It takes us a long time to realize that Christianity is a life-and-death situation. It takes longer to believe that we are not capable of directing our own lives. It takes even more time to realize that we're "by nature children of wrath" and that if we continue to drift, we are going over the falls!

It is "natural" to be lost. It is natural to be selfish. It is natural to be lazy. It is natural to be naive, especially if you are a woman. It is unnatural to be a worthy woman or a worthy man.

∼ SENSIBLE ABOUT TIME

"Plan your day or lose it." Do not be ruled by the urgent! I am convinced that one of the hardest daily tasks we have is conscientiously getting our priorities straight. God knows what this day should and will hold.

Emergencies arise when the urgent must be served. But usually a day can be planned and your objectives carried out. We need to assign ourselves three good-sized tasks for the day. Reasonable tasks. Then do them.

"Time is like a weaver's shuttle." We think the babies will stay babies, but they don't, and before we know it, they are being married. You have heard the old saying: "The road to hell is paved with good intentions."

We mean to get around to training our children, keeping our romance alive, and nurturing our children in the way of the Lord. Then we sit in shock as they parade in their cap and gown.

Procrastination is a deadly vice. To put off until tomorrow what needs to be done today is slow suicide. Immaturity says, "You have a lifetime." Maturity says, "Life is short, and you are living now." God says, "I might come today."

> Lord, make me to know my end, and what is the extent of my days; let me know how transient I am. Behold, You have made my days as handbreadths, and my lifetime as nothing in Your sight; surely, every man at his best is a mere breath. Surely every man walks about as a phantom (Ps. 39:4–6).
>
> This is the beginning of a new day. God has given me this day to use as I will. I can waste it or use it for good. What I do today is very important because I am exchanging a day of my life for it. When tomorrow comes, this day will be gone forever . . . I shall not regret the price I paid for it.[32]

We may think we have more time than money. We may have more money. "Redeem the time" (Eph. 5:16 KJV). Buy it. Use it. There are jobs today that must be done or prices to pay for them left undone.

SENSIBLE ABOUT MONEY

Many of us are uncomfortable with the verse that says, "A fool and his money are soon parted." Nor do we cherish the old saying that "money burns a hole in our pocket." Yet, we would all agree that mature people should be wiser spenders than the immature.

God loves to say yes. He wants us to have our heart's desires in time—in His time. He tells us how much better He can give gifts than we can to our children. When we look back at the patriarchs of the Old Testament, we find some to be very wealthy men.

The book of Job was written to show us that a good man can have bad things happen to him, and he can lose his wealth and health.

It was a belief at that time that good health and wealth were given only to good men and that bad things happened only to bad people. It is still generally true that blessings come with a consecrated life. We must always remember the end of the Lord. Job was saved and his fortunes restored; even doubled.

> God loves to give, for He is the great giver. God is love, and love gives and gives. But God has a plan for His giving, and we need to find and execute His plan. His will is for us to give as we are prospered, and then He will give it back pressed down and running over (1 Cor. 16:2; 2 Cor. 9:7; Luke 6:38). This has always been a principle of God's law, both to the Jew and to the Christian.

> He throws out the challenge under the old law:

> "Bring the whole tithe into the storehouse, so that there may be food in My house, and test Me now in this," says the Lord of hosts, "if I will not open for you the windows of heaven, and pour out for you a blessing until it overflows" (Mal. 3:10).

God says, "You give first, and then I will give back." That takes faith. "I'll pour out generously," says the Lord. When Christians come to me with financial problems, I always ask first, "How is your giving?" Usually the solution to their problem is in their answer.

Sometimes it is not in the giving but in the using. We by nature want too much too soon. It would not be good for us to get things too soon because the human being is never satisfied.

"He who loves money will not be satisfied with money, nor he who loves abundance with its income. This too is vanity" (Eccles. 5:10). "You cannot serve God and money," the New Testament teaches in Luke 16:13.

God wants to gradually take us into a blessed world as we become more blessed people. We upset His plan when both the parents have to be busy making money, and the children suffer for it. Maturity sees this, but naivete and selfishness want it all now. The price is too steep!

◈ SENSIBLE ABOUT GOOD COMPANIONS

"Birds of a feather flock together." We tend to choose for friends those we like rather than those we would be like. Our criteria for their being a part of our lives is: Do they make us laugh? Do we have about the same finances? Do we like the same people? Are our husbands pleased with their husbands? Are we compatible? (Note that we haven't mentioned spirituality!) Do they make us better people when we are together? Are they really striving to please God? Do they take seriously the proper raising of their children? Do I admire them for their goodness?

"Do not be deceived: 'Bad company corrupts good morals'" (1 Cor. 15:33). When running with the wrong crowd, we have to gradually change our close friends. Some friends are too expensive, spiritually speaking. They bring out the worst in us. We tend to be lax where they are lax. They tempt us to worldliness. We cannot afford them.

A sweet Christian lady gave us this saying once at a ladies' day, and I treasure it.

> A rule to govern my life: Anything that dims my vision of Christ or takes away my taste for Bible study or cramps my prayer life or makes Christian work difficult is wrong for me, I must, as a Christian, turn away from it.

The book of Proverbs has so much to say about the danger of bad companions and how this relationship can even cause death. How many sweet young people got in the wrong crowd and didn't live long enough to be conscious of the danger? Legions. Immaturity doesn't recognize the danger of the wrong associations. Immature people feel that they are in control when they are not.

No human body can allow drugs, alcohol, promiscuous sex, abuse of the body, and abuse of the mind to have control without paying the piper. Maturity knows that payday is coming, but the grasshopper continues to exult in the warmth of summer.

We need to seek out the best there are in the church where we meet. God tells us to appreciate our elders. He puts the responsibility on us to seek them out and esteem them. First Thessalonians 5:12–13 says,

> But we request of you, brethren, that you appreciate those who diligently labor among you, and have charge over you in the Lord and give you instructions, and that you esteem them very highly in love because of their work. Live in peace with one another.

God tells us to call the most righteous for prayer when we have sick ones, for God is nearer to the most righteous.

> Is anyone among you sick? Then he must call for the elders of the church, and they are to pray over him, anointing him with oil in the name of the Lord; and the prayer offered in faith will restore the one who is sick, and the Lord will raise him up, and if he has committed sins, they will be forgiven him. Therefore, confess your sins to one another, and pray for one another, so that you may be healed. The effective prayer of a righteous man can accomplish much (James 5:14–16).

If you are a younger woman, seek out the godly older women for advice. Become dear friends. Get involved in their lives for your own good. If you are an older godly woman, keep your latch string off and your telephone ready for their ring. You may help to save a soul, a family.

Watch your TV companions. You will learn to emulate the wicked woman if you are not careful. Watch your reading companions. There are both kinds. There are some new books you have to burn and some programs that you must turn off.

✑ A WINNER OF SOULS

"He that winneth souls is wise" (Prov. 11:30 KJV). There are those who feel no compulsion to win souls. They excuse themselves because they have young children, or they don't know enough to try to teach others, or God doesn't expect them to win souls but to just please their husbands.

Then there is the other extreme. "I am commanded to win souls, so I am justified to leave my children, neglect my house, be so busy serving God that I am released from my home commitments."

Either extreme is wrong. The happy medium is that God does expect a woman to put her family and home first. Neglected children and dirty houses are abhorrent to God as well as to the world. These actions cause God to be blasphemed rather than glorified. I heard a godly man say, "When a woman is changing her baby's diaper, she is doing the work of the Lord." That's true.

But am I excluded from personal work until my children are grown? Certainly not. Jesus set the example that we must be about our Father's business. There are times we can have our Bible study no matter what the ages of the children. There are occasions when we can attend a ladies day, gospel meeting, or ladies' classes. There are times we can sit beside a friend and open our Bibles together, and we can teach a person how to become a Christian. But these will have to be planned times.

In a locality where I used to live, the ladies met one day a week and went out to do personal work. Some of the older ladies babysat for the younger ones. This gave the young mothers a chance to be out and away from their responsibilities for a while. They went to see other young mothers and talked with them and taught them.

If you have children who are very young but are on a workable schedule where you can put them to bed early, then you can have a couple in for social times and for Bible studies. We used to spend many hours like this with other young couples. This way we didn't have to pay a sitter, and we were close to the children if we were needed.

"First a friend and then a brother" is the saying we have written on our church stationery. It is the most successful way to teach. People have to know you before they will let you teach them. Eating together is such a good way for the beginning of personal work. We have had more success with that approach than any other in the mission fields of New England, and I believe that it will work everywhere. "Becoming all things to all men" starts with getting to know them.

These "couple" nights are also important to your marriage. The pulling together in the yoke of marriage takes a lot of practice. It gives much happiness and contentment at the end of the evening to know that you were allowed to do something for Him. It makes your life happier and your love grow for your spouse who has the same ideals.

ᘒ Becoming a Realist

God wants us to leave naivete and become adults, and this means becoming realists. Jesus knew what was in the heart of man. Do we expect every Christian to act like one? Do we unrealistically demand perfection of every or any older Christian?

Dale Carnegie in his book, *How to Win Friends and Influence People*, tells us that though we expect people to act unemotionally and wisely, we are all unpredictable. We are all the product of our natural-born temperaments, environments, schools, churches, books we have read, shows we've seen—everything we have contacted.

Who says what's normal and to be expected? God takes us where He finds us and tries to bring us with our individual potentialities to where He wants us. He wants us to die to self and become like Him. Too often we are offended if we feel another is not as serious as we are about this Christian life. We quickly become judgmental and mark that person off. But God is a realist. He knows the heart, thoughts, the background, and potential, and He judges impartially. We have to learn to do the same.

God commands us to love even if the object of our love does not love us. We have only to answer for ourselves, so we should pray for them when they do not love us. We must continue to strive to be lovable.

Pure religion is hard to come by. It means loving the unlovable. It means helping the ones we would rather not help. It means foot-washing. It means work. We excuse ourselves and others who draw back from service, but that is immaturity. Really, it's just sin.

James 2 tells us of our putting down the poor man and elevating the rich one. "But you have dishonored the poor man . . . But if you show partiality, you are committing sin and are convicted by the law as transgressors" (James 2:6–9).

We tend to feel a "sistership" for those who think as we do, dress as we do, live as we live—but only for them. We are in the danger of being Pharisees, unknowingly, by wanting to teach others just like us and then have them feel the same way we do about the same people.

We can no more pick our family in God than we can in the flesh. Christ died for all, and the acceptance of His blood and forgiveness gives us a blood relationship with God's family.

"How long will you love being simple?" God asks us. In time, may we maturely answer, "Let me see things as they really are and learn to love as You do."

⇾⟫⟫ HELP ME TO GROW UP ⟪⟪⟪⇽

In the bitter waves of woe,
Beaten and tossed about
By the sullen winds that blow
From the desolate shores of doubt,
Where the anchors that faith had cast
Are dragging in the gale,
I am quietly holding fast
To the things that cannot fail.

—Washington Gladden[33]

A Fearsome Passage

There are some scary scriptures in God's Word—scriptures that strike fear in all of us. At least I feel that way. Here is one, and it is so fitting for what we are discussing—wisdom and being sensible. Solomon wrote, "The wise woman builds her house, but the foolish tears it down with her own hands" (Prov. 14:1).

Since Solomon was an expert when it came to women—700 wives and 300 concubines—his observances of women probably included seeing this proverb acted out in real life. That is somewhat frightening to me because I can see how easy it would be to tear down my own house. I have seen it happen. An insensible woman, a greedy woman, an uncaring woman digs and digs at her own foundation, shoveling all alone, dismantling brick by brick until her home collapses. And there is nothing left but sadness and ruin. Think of the husband. Think of the children. Think of her.

Seriously Sensible

God our Father gave Titus a list of seven qualities He wants young women to possess, and *sensible (sober-minded)* is number three on the list. If God takes the time to warn us about being foolish and its consequences, and if God takes the time to warn us about a foolish woman and a wise woman, then we need to wake up and smell the coffee. God is trying to tell us something. May we beware of being that foolish, senseless woman, and instead be the woman who takes God seriously, takes loving her husband seriously, takes raising her children seriously, takes the gospel of Jesus Christ seriously, and takes her role as queen of the home seriously. After all, do any of us really want to lose our precious husband and family, and then God?

⌒ A WOMAN'S PRAYER ⌒

Holy Father, we praise Your wondrous name and power. Thank You from the bottom of our hearts for loving us. We don't deserve Your love and help. Please help us to want to learn and grow and change into the daughters You have designed. Please help us to be sensible and wise women—not foolish daughters. We know that the impossible is possible with You, Father. Please show us how to be better daughters. We love You so much. In Jesus' name we pray, Amen.

THOUGHT QUESTIONS

1. Why are we tempted to stay naive?
2. How do naivete and selfishness upset God's plan for the home?
3. How can we maturely do better with our time?
4. Why is the choosing of our companions so important?
5. How does one get godly wisdom? Read James 1:5.

♪ **Song:** "Have Thine Own Way, Lord"

Insights

Our Sisters' Voices

Have you ever personally experienced a Titus 2 woman who took you under her wing and nurtured you? I thought you might like to read some true accounts from our sisters in the faith who have experienced this relationship. Here are their stories.

My husband Shane's grandmother, Pat, was a huge encouragement to me spiritually. Before I was a Christian and while I was engaged to Shane, Pat would always talk to me about spiritual things and invited me to attend a marriage seminar with her, which I did. I went to church with Shane and his family on Sundays and loved God but had gotten comfortable, not really thinking about the fact that I still wasn't a Christian as God teaches us in the Bible. I needed guidance. After Shane and I married, Pat would pick me up once a week and bring me with her to a local Bible study up the street. She was always thinking about my soul. Her Christian example of always reaching out to me, along with her steadfastness throughout all of the great trials in her life, had an enormous impact on me spiritually; one that I will be forever grateful for. She played a big part in my becoming a Christian as well as staying strong and focusing on God. I love and miss her very much."

—Paula

❦❦❦

I was a newly baptized mother of one who found her way. My initial "seeking" was driven by this little one of mine just two years old. It was my responsibility to teach him about the Lord. Right? Right, so I tried to go back to my Catholic roots. My memories, for the most part, were of special times with my Memere (grandmother). Even though every time I looked backward she would whip my eyes front. I did like the wonder of the church building and of course dressing up. Finding this revisit to be unfulfilling, I knew it wasn't for us. Oh but God!

Soon after that, a friend dropped by my workplace to apply for a job. We reminisced some, and before she left she handed me a tract and an invitation to come to church. I didn't read it right away, but when I did, it directed me to reach out to her and set up a study. Every Tuesday night for three months. My first anchor. At the studies, my questions were met with, "Let's see what the Bible has to say about it." Another anchor.

I started going to every study and service. The women all embraced my coming to worship and showed me the meaning of being the body of Christ. A couple of women led me to teach. Oh, the important roles of teachers. First they offered to take my son to class. He was a bit clingy so I became the "seatbelt" that kept him in the chair. I learned so much sitting in that toddlers' class. Another anchor. The hospitality was warm. Potlucks, studies, ladies' classes. I grew—my son grew and before I knew it, I was teaching. Me teaching. Another anchor. From the sister that handed me the tract, to the body of Christian women showing me Christ, and the Sunday school teachers that molded me to do the same—some of my many anchors. I'm so thankful.

—Jan

M y parents became Christians when I was a baby. An older couple at church studied with them and became my "adopted grandparents." I even called them Grandma Betty and Pap Fred. They were always there for my family for any and all kinds of needs. They treated us like we were part of their family and they were part of mine. They had us over for dinner more times than I can count; our families went camping together for many years; they came to family reunions with us; when I was nine, my grandfather passed away suddenly, and Grandma Betty and Pap Fred took the time to drive over two hours to be at his funeral with us. We spent many special occasions together. They encouraged us in any way they could. Grandma Betty was a woman of many talents. She taught me to cook, bake, and make fudge and other treats. She cut and permed my hair, my mom's hair, and cut my brother's hair. She baked special birthday cakes, such as an ambulance cake for my brother and a doll cake for me. She sewed a special doll for me that I played with until I was too old for it. She spent time with me and gave me advice when I needed it. I knew I could trust her and go to her with anything. I loved sitting with her in church on Sunday mornings and Sunday nights. There is one thing that I am especially thankful for. She taught me to make homemade communion bread. She prepared communion most Sundays and she shared that important task with me. I am so grateful that God put a godly woman in my life to show me His love and teach me life lessons that I may not have otherwise learned. Her faithfulness, support, encouragement, and love meant so much to me as a child, teenager, and adult. Grandma Betty was a very special lady.

—Kim

~eಲ Qಲ~

My siblings and I were raised by my grandparents, since the oldest was eight years old and the youngest eighteen months old. They weren't "church goers," so it was junior high before I started attending church. First, I went to the Baptist church. Then the church of Christ started a bussing program and I had several ladies who taught me and influenced me during my school years. I don't want to name them because I don't want to leave any one out, but they know who they were. They were ladies of the church: school teacher's wife, farmers' wives, and more. But one woman really studied with me and taught me the plan of salvation and what God required of me. She helped me a lot. Then I graduated, married, had kids, and then nineteen-and-a-half years later divorced. Before things started really going downhill fast, I met the then-current preacher's wife. The first visit I knew she was coming to "get on to me" for not being in church and having my kids in church. But even though I knew why she was there, she was the sweetest lady I had ever met. I tried to go to church more often and live better. My husband was a truck driver, so it was really up to me alone to get there. Sometimes I did better than others but Liz Hendry never gave up on me. She was always the sweetest friend and best encourager. And most important, she was a teacher I could have never dreamed to have. She talked in ways that made me more than glad to listen. She never once reprimanded me. She grew to be my Miss Liz very quickly and helped me to be the Christian that I needed to be. She can tell you that it took, and sometimes still takes, a lot of training.

Not only did she teach me from the Bible (we had Bible study in and out of church), but by example. Seeing her in action has been my biggest influence because learning the word, what it says: that is one thing. But if you're blessed enough to have someone in your life that knows the word and lives it every day—now that's when you know you are blessed.

I pray for another day with her in my life so I can continue to love her and learn from her. Sometimes she probably wonders, but believe you me, I am taking lessons from her every day. She has taught me so much about being a Christian wife, and even a grandparent. She shares her kindness, life experiences, and most important, her Christian love and knowledge just by being her. She always says, "Think about this." And when it comes to my grandparenting skills she says, "Always talk to them—about any and every thing." My prayer is to never forget any of her life's lessons or her Bible lessons. Every day I pray for another day to have her influence.

Without her in my life the last 25-plus years, there's no telling where or who I would be.

—Diana

ကလေ

A few years ago, just after I turned fifty, a good friend started a ladies' class with our church home school group. I was the oldest of the group with a grown daughter and a grandson. It was my twelve-year-old homeschooled son that categorized me to be in this group. Close behind me in age was my friend Kelly who had five children ranging from ages two to thirteen. Kelly had made the effort to organize this class, but she recognized that I was the experienced older woman of the group and encouraged me to lead it with her. Sometimes we need a gentle push because we don't recognize our own qualifications.

I don't know exactly when it happened, but somewhere along the way my image of myself as the young struggling mom gave way to that of an older woman with experience and wisdom who had many life-lessons of value to share. That push led me into a new season of life that I now embrace. It was so refreshing to see a group of young moms sincerely dedicated to rearing their children to please God—they were not just going through the motions of living every day to get by. Early on, they had been taught to consult God's Word daily for direction while their children were young. And they also had one another to lean on.

I have since moved and see a need in the current congregation. About seven families have children under five, and I have started a mentoring/support group/class. One other older mom and I plan to host a dinner followed by a class for the young moms once a month and use your mom's book *Precious Are God's Plans* for the class portion. We're hoping the young moms will form a bond as sisters in Christ who will be raising their children together until adulthood. (Which you and I know will come quicker than they'll ever realize.) I pray that their experience will be similar to that of my first group

I want God to use me and make me a good mentor and servant to these girls. I see such a contrast in what the world wants to teach these moms and what God wants them to learn. I pray their hearts will be open. (By the way, we were going to start this young moms' class in March but COVID stopped us.) We recently got the go ahead from the elders to begin. Satan may have gotten us to delay by seven months, but we already know God wins the battle. So now we are more determined for a successful ministry!

—Mary

I asked two of my mom's best friends, Liz and Fran, to tell all of us what it was like to have Mom, Lea Fowler, in their life and what kind of influence she had. Let's listen to what these older women have to say.

As a preacher's wife of forty-five years, faces from the past fill my mind with memories of so many wonderful women and their love and devotion to our Lord. But there is one of these women who is always a constant in my thoughts.

I met Lea Fowler in New England years ago and my life was never the same again. She could be like a beautiful spring day or a winter storm ready to blow in. No matter which, God was always the subject. She had such a way that you never wanted to miss a thing she said, and I never wanted our visits to end. I always wanted to be a better person after being with her. I was blessed to have her friendship and guidance many years. Those of you who read this, I pray you have a forever friend like Lea.

—Liz

Lea entered my life, the most fascinating person I've ever known! She loved the Lord more than anyone I knew; she loved the word of God and knew how to teach it; she loved the lost and never missed an opportunity to reach them and yet she was so funny, and I loved being with her. We started marking our Bibles with the eight lessons she and Russ used for second teaching. And then I would teach my husband Ken the lesson we just had. And so it began, many years of studying, searching, praying, crying, and loving, serving our Savior. Over sixty years to be exact!

Becky, you asked me what it was like to be on the phone so much with your mom. It was amazing, therapeutic, spiritual, and uplifting. Remember I had two little ones and later, three that kept me hopping. We never shied away from controversial subjects. The tougher the better. Also we talked about you! A lot! Along with your brother and sister, as we did my family. We came to love each of our families like our own and their spiritual lives were of utmost importance.

—Fran

CHASTE, *Not Chased*

"Pure"

Tell me about the day you were born into this world. What was it like? Okay, I know—you don't remember. Neither do I. You and I were babies and we didn't know anything. We were helpless and completely dependent on others.

Tell me about your second birth—the day you were baptized into Jesus. What was it like? Now, this you do remember. I do too. You and I were not helpless babies but of a responsible and accountable age. We knew what we were doing. We knew what sin was, and we knew we had committed it. We wanted to be clean again, forgiven of our sins, and we wanted to go to heaven. We obeyed the gospel call of Jesus. How did we do that?

- ✤ We believed: "Therefore I said to you that you will die in your sins; for unless you believe that I am He, you will die in your sins" (John 8:24).

- ✤ We repented: "I tell you, no, but unless you repent, you will all likewise perish" (Luke 13:3).

- ✤ We confessed: "Therefore everyone who confesses Me before men, I will also confess him before My Father who is in heaven" (Matt. 10:32).

❖ We were baptized: "Now when they heard this, they were pierced to the heart, and said to Peter and the rest of the apostles, 'Brethren, what shall we do?' Peter said to them, 'Repent, and each of you be baptized in the name of Jesus Christ for the forgiveness of your sins; and you will receive the gift of the Holy Spirit'" (Acts 2:37–38).

Is that all there is to being a Christian? No, it's just the beginning of the most wonderful life one could live. John wrote in Revelation 2:10, "Be faithful until death, and I will give you the crown of life." Go back to that most important moment of your life and reflect for a second or two. Do you remember coming up out of the watery grave of baptism? Do you remember that feeling of being pure?

A New Beginning

When we obey the gospel and are baptized, we are as pure as the day we entered this life as a crying infant. Our sins are washed away, and we become a new creature, forgiven, a child of God, and free from sin. We are given the opportunity to begin again. Even though it was some sixty years ago that I was baptized, I still remember vividly how marvelous it felt to be washed clean from my sins. My dad baptized me in a cool New England river on a Sunday afternoon in July. It was a wonderful moment, even though I truly believe Dad held me under at least thirty minutes!

As Christians who have been washed in the blood of Jesus and forgiven, we know that we will sin again. Is there no hope for us? Oh, there is definitely hope. We can have a blank slate, a new beginning with our heavenly Father every day: "But if we walk in the Light as He Himself is in the Light, we have fellowship with one another, and the blood of Jesus His Son cleanses us from all sin" (1 John 1:7). Notice in this verse that walking in the light keeps us in the right relationship with God, and Jesus' blood that we touched in baptism keeps on cleansing us. It is necessary to always do His will and keep walking with Him in order to have the continual cleansing. Yes, we will still make mistakes, but our sins will be forgiven as we repent and do right.

⤜≫≫⤛ PAUSE AND PONDER ⤜≪≪⤛

Tell of your baptism. What convicted you? What do you remember? Who influenced you to take that step? How do you know that even as a Christian, you will sin? Provide scripture. How are we assured of continual cleansing from sin?

It's Tough!

This chapter is tough for many of us to grasp. It is hard for me to write it. Why is it so difficult? Because being pure and right and holy is such a challenge for any Christian to begin with. But this passage in Titus specifically admonishes the young woman to be pure. Pure in mind. Pure in actions. Pure in speech. Pure in all things. And none of this is easy for us. Why? Be honest now, girls, we know what we are. We know our mistakes, and we know our faults. Often we are too hard on ourselves, thinking God could not really love us the way we are. Nothing is further from the truth. God does love us, has always loved us and sent His marvelous Son to erase all those sins of ours and help us to change. We believe being pure is impossible—but remember, girls, "with God all things are possible" (Matt. 19:26).

What is it to be pure or chaste? Wayne Jackson defines chaste as "pure in all areas of life-habits, dress, language, etc."[34]

Consider the following input about purity.

> When I became a Christian, I thought I was so holy. Actually, I felt holy. Then the day came when I discovered that thoughts can be sinful. At that point, I learned that I was not nearly as holy as I had previously believed. In fact, I was continuing to sin greatly against God.
>
> The Greek word translated "to be pure" in Titus 2 is *hagnos,* which means to be "free from ceremonial defilement; holy; sacred; chaste;

pure; free from sin; and innocent." This word is similar to the word *hagios* which is often translated "holy." This righteous purity is not only outward chastity but also inward freedom from impure thoughts.

Often bondage to sinful lust is thought to be a problem for men but not women. That is not true. Women also may be enticed into the world of fantasies, self-gratification, pornography, and immorality. It all begins with their thoughts.[35]

Frank Chesser says:

> A marriage partner's conduct with members of the opposite sex should be above reproach. When separated, there should be no doubt in either spouse's mind as to the deportment of the other. All conversation and body language should conform to the highest standard of purity, faithfulness, and love for one's husband or wife. Paul cautioned Timothy to treat "the older women as mothers, and the younger women as sisters, in all purity" (1 Tim. 5:2). There is no area of life fraught with more opportunities for Satan to work marital and spiritual ruin than interactions between the sexes. Thinking right about God and one's mate will not permit any form of conduct to infringe upon the marriage relationship that diminishes trust and sows seeds of doubt. Flirting should be reserved for teenagers."[36]

Even more important than man's wisdom is the Lord's wisdom. What does God say?

- "How can a young man keep his way pure? By keeping *it* according to Your word" (Ps. 119:9).
- "Now flee from youthful lusts and pursue righteousness, faith, love *and* peace, with those who call on the Lord from a pure heart " (2 Tim. 2:22).

The Key Is in Thinking

"How do I get a pure heart; how do I keep my way pure; how do I change my ways?" you may ask. Mom once quipped, "What we think, we are. What do we think about all day? Great thoughts make great people, and pygmy thoughts make pygmies." Are you thinking great thoughts about Bible examples and truths?

The magnificent excerpt below is a command. I urge all of us to read it; memorize it; write it on our hearts; absorb it; live it.

> Finally, brethren, whatever is true, whatever is honorable, whatever is right, whatever is pure, whatever is lovely, whatever is of good repute, if there is any excellence and if anything worthy of praise, dwell on these things. The things you have learned and received and heard and seen in me, practice these things, and the God of peace will be with you (Phil. 4:8–9).

Do you see the word *dwell* here in this NASB translation? God doesn't tell us to just glance at a few good qualities, or to even just look at them once in a while. But God tells us to let our minds dwell—meditate—on these things. Dwelling takes time. Since the word *dwell* is part of the word *dwelling*, a place where we live, doesn't it make sense to let God's Word live in us, too? And take up residence in us? Let's take up this challenge the Lord issues us and think about godly things, and in turn, practice them. The end result? Our God, the God of peace, will be with us. What do you really want in this life—peace or conflict? I will take peace every time.

Has it occurred to you that where your mind dwells shows up on your face? Mom thought so.

> Women are especially mindful of their faces. We need to recognize that good thoughts make us beautiful. Lovely thoughts make us lovely. I've heard it said that we cannot help what we look like before we are forty, but we can help what we look like after that. That saying is emphasizing that our thoughts show in our face. Euripides said, "It's not beauty but fine qualities, my girl, that keep a husband."
>
> "Dwell on these things" (Phil. 4:8). Is it honorable, the thought I just had? If so, dwell on that thought. Is it a good report? If not, put it out. Is it an excellent thought and one of praise? Keep thinking about that. Exchange the bad thought for the excellent one. This is the power of positive thinking taught by the original Teacher.

How simple the teaching and how hard to discipline our minds to the task! We must learn the art of self-defense. We must learn to love ourselves enough to protect our minds against the wiles of Satan. He bombards our minds with what is false, dishonorable, unjust, impure, and ugly. These things are not worth thinking about and cannot be praised. That is his list, and we must not be ignorant of his devices.[37]

Mom continued,

Note the word *practice* in Philippians 4:9. Put into practice what you have learned and what you are learning. Could we find the courage to stop the unlovely talking among the sisters who will not pass the above tests? Could we say something kind and honorable and gracious?

The Bible tells us to "set our affections on things that are above." Deliberately set or place your mind on things above, and don't let it get off the track. Satan will see to it that the constant temptation is there to think about the unloveliness in life and in the church, for they are many.[38]

A fitting scripture that coincides with Philippians 4:8 is David's remarkable Psalm 119:11: "Your word I have treasured in my heart, that I may not sin against You." Only by meditating upon God's precious Word was David able to prevent sinful thoughts, and we know David was far from perfect. That same Word can do the identical thing for us today. As Christians we often say, "We are in the world but not of the world" and "where our treasure is there our heart is." Let's examine what Matthew was inspired to write:

After Jesus called the crowd to Him, He said to them, "Hear and understand. It is not what enters into the mouth that defiles the man, but what proceeds out of the mouth, this defiles the man" (Matt. 15:10–11).

What are we putting into our brains? We can certainly count on those thoughts to pour out of our mouths. Dwell on the Word; treasure the Word and learn to be pure. It is possible. As my mom says later in this chapter, "By filling our minds with His word, we become like Him, and our old life cannot move back in."

Who Sins?

Everybody. A few people believe they never do any wrong. We know that isn't true. First John 1:8 says: "If we say that we have no sin, we are deceiving ourselves and the truth is not in us." We must learn to recognize sin, and that can take time. A dear friend gave me this description of sin: "At first we abhor it; then we endure it; and at last we embrace it."

We Christians need to look ourselves in the eye and admit that we still battle sin. Many days are a struggle with a "heap of problems." It's true! We hope no one ever knows certain facts about our past or the sin that so easily entangles us. But we must learn to forgive ourselves. Jesus has! To be converted means we are changed, and because of God's wondrous grace we can look forward to heaven with Him.

> *We no longer walk in the flesh, sinning deliberately, but now we walk with Jesus.*

We are not the same sinner anymore. We no longer walk in the flesh, sinning deliberately, but now we walk with Jesus, obeying the Word that God has given us. That is the Christian walk. And that walk must be absolutely and unequivocally made with just one book in our hands and hearts—the Bible, the Word of God. God has so masterfully laid out all the instructions for the life He wants for us. It is up to us to decide if we are going to open The Book and find the answers and the help we always need. The Lord will show us through His Word how to stay strong and use the mind He has given us for good and pure things, not sinful and wicked things. A preacher once said that God has only one goal and that is for His children to look like Him! And isn't that our goal too?

Fix Your Eyes

Listen, my sisters, God knows all things. And He knows us. He knows what makes us stumble, and He is always there helping us to run from sin and be that pure, discreet, chaste woman too. The Hebrews writer said it so succinctly when he wrote:

> Therefore, since we have so great a cloud of witnesses surrounding us, let us also lay aside every encumbrance and the sin which so easily entangles us, and let us run with endurance the race that is set before us, fixing our eyes on Jesus, the author and perfecter of faith, who for the joy set before Him endured the cross, despising the shame, and has sat down at the right hand of the throne of God (Heb. 12:1–2).

Fixing our eyes on Jesus is always the answer to changing anything. If we are to ever be able to look like Him, then it is a given that we must be in God's Word constantly. Where else am I going to find out what Jesus is like? This is where the life of Jesus, His ministry, and His behavior are revealed.

We must not only read the Bible but also study it, dig deeply, and examine it. Ponder the words, the accounts, the people, and the truths God puts forth. The Word changes us. And that is conversion! We become changed women—daughters striving to be all that we can be for our Father. Don't look back. Don't look to the left or to the right. Just look up to the Lord.

Most of us care about how the world sees us. We want to be viewed as accomplished, stable, and knowledgeable Christian women when the truth is, many days are tough. We may feel inadequate, unstable, and weak in the faith. If you feel this way, my sister, don't despair. We are all in the same boat.

Mom often instructed me in Jesus' words, "So do not worry about tomorrow; for tomorrow will care for itself. Each day has enough trouble of its own" (Matt. 6:34). She then quoted the King James Version ending: "Sufficient unto the day is the evil thereof." Mom wisely concluded, "Notice the word *evil* here. Becky, you will have many days in your life that will be nothing but pure evil because Satan is doing everything he can to make you fall."

I must tell you that she was so right. I have lived many years—yes, I am old—and I can attest to the fact that there have been quite a few days that were horrible, devastating, miserable, and stamped all over with evil—all hurled my way by Satan to destroy me or my family. But my Father stepped in, delivered me, and said, "Trust in [Me] with all your heart, and do not lean on your own understanding" (Prov. 3:5). Every. Single. Time.

PAUSE AND PONDER

Stop whatever you are doing, my sister, get your Bible out and turn to Isaiah 46:3–4. God speaks seriously to His children—the Jews and the remnant of Israel. Read it aloud, then circle the word *you*. Now read it again, and replace *you* with your name.

LISTEN TO ME, O HOUSE OF JACOB,

And all the remnant of the house of Israel,
You who have been borne by Me from birth
And have been carried from the womb;
Even to your old age I will be the same,
And even to your graying years I will bear you!
I have done it, and I will carry you;
And I will bear you and I will deliver you.

—Isaiah 46:3–4

He Will Carry You

Christians are now a part of the remnant of the house of Israel. We know that we have been grafted into the tree, the people of Israel. (Read

Romans 11.) Isaiah 46:3–4 gives those who are Christians such comfort, knowing that God has cared for us from the time we were in our mother's womb, through our teenage years, and now in our gray-haired years. God has never stopped caring for us, and He has never ceased reaching down into our messed-up lives and delivering us from Satan's trickery. My sweet sisters, please don't forget Isaiah 46:3–4. Underline it and share it with others. It gives us great comfort knowing God has never stopped working in our lives. And never forget this: God certainly knows every trick Satan has up his sleeve. Trust in God; He always wins. Take time to write down the times that God has delivered you. Write down scriptures that bring you comfort, beginning with Exodus 14:14.

> *God certainly knows every trick Satan has up his sleeve. Trust in God.*

We must recognize the fact that Satan works overtime to make us sin, stumble, and give up. We all have a past and a present and a future. So did those men who walked with Jesus daily. Question: Did they have forgiveness and hope of salvation? Of course they did, and so do we. The Father has given us a brain to make the right decisions and also to rest assured of His promises. One of those promises is that He will never forsake us. He is always right by our side as we fight sin and temptation. God is always there. Look at these marvelous passages that give us confidence in our Father:

- Psalm 56:11: "In God I have put my trust, I shall not be afraid. What can man do to me?"

- Psalm 118:6: "The Lord is for me; I will not fear; What can man do to me?"

- Hebrews 13:5–6: "Make sure that your character is free from the love of money, being content with what you have; for He Himself has said, 'I will never desert you, nor will I ever forsake you,' so that we confidently say, 'The Lord is my helper, I will not be afraid. What will man do to me?'"

❖ 1 Corinthians 10:13: "No temptation has overtaken you but such as is common to man; and God is faithful, who will not allow you to be tempted beyond what you are able, but with the temptation will provide the way of escape also, so that you will be able to endure it."

MOM SAYS

✐ PRACTICE THESE THINGS

"Blessed are the pure in heart for they shall see God" (Matt. 5:8). What a promise! If we are pure in heart, we shall see God face to face "and tell the story saved by grace." It is not normal or natural to be pure in heart. This wonderful characteristic is learned.

In climbing the Christian ladder described in 2 Peter 1:5–7, we start with faith. Faith is the foundation of Christianity. The first thing we add to our faith is virtue. Some versions say "goodness" or "you must work hard to be good" or "goodness of life." One writer defined virtue as, "Clean up your life." That definition has always stuck in my mind.

Now that you have faith, clean up your life. Throw out the trash. Discard the things that make you stumble. It takes a long time to know all that makes you fall. We can in good conscience do a lot of things as a new Christian that we will not be able to justify as an older one. Many things look acceptable to our young eyes that are not pleasing in God's eyes.

At the conclusion of this list of qualities to add to your life, there is a little phrase that is very potent. It says, "For as long as you practice these things you will never stumble" (2 Pet. 1:10).

Practice is the key to godly living, Study for knowledge; pray for wisdom; and practice what you are learning. You start out with the milk of the word, the part that is easily understood and digested, and you grow gradually until you can eat the meat. "But solid food is for the mature, who because of practice have their senses trained to discern good and evil" (Heb. 5:14).

We are constantly adding virtue, cleaning up our lives, practicing what God teaches us is good. His list is different from ours, but in time, as we become like Him, our list agrees. We become pure in His sight, and we shall see Him if we remain that way.

Why is it so much worse to see a bad woman than a bad man? Why do dirty words or profanity seem so much harsher coming from her lips than his? Why do we hope for women to be ladies when they are not?

I've heard it said, "Man was made from dust and woman was made from his rib so she is twice refined." Or, "God said it was not good for man to be alone, but after He made woman He said, 'It is very good.'" Mankind expects more from women than men though we are expecting less from women as the days go by. (This is sad for womankind and for mankind.)

God gives us examples of both good and bad women. "This is the way of an adulterous woman: she eats and wipes her mouth, and says, 'I have done no wrong'" (Prov. 30:20).

When we think of the woman who is pure in heart and whom we want to emulate, our thoughts go back to the worthy woman.

> Her children rise up and bless her; Her husband also, and he praises her saying: "Many daughters have done nobly, but you excel them all." Charm is deceitful and beauty is vain, but a woman who fears the Lord, she shall be praised. Give her the product of her hands, and let her work praise her in the gates (Prov. 31:28–31).

Of all people who praise us, whom would we rather hear it from—the world or our family? Our family knows us. There are few masks worn in the house. Our family means the most to us. They are bone of our bone. They hold our heart. Did you notice that they "rise up" when they bless her? Not a casual looking up from a book with a

"Good job, Mom," as they return to their pleasure, but a stopping and rising and a blessing because she deserves it.

THE KEY TO BEAUTY

God stresses to the women how to look physically: "Likewise, I want women to adorn themselves with proper clothing, modestly and discreetly, not with braided hair and gold or pearls or costly garments" (1 Tim. 2:9). The Phillips translation says it this way,

> Similarly, the women should be dressed neatly, their adornment being modesty and serious mindedness. It is not for them to have an elaborate hairstyle, jewelry of gold or pearls, or expensive clothes, but as becomes women who profess to believe in God, it is for them to show their faith by the way they live. A woman should live quietly and humbly (1 Tim. 2:9–11).

Be neat; be modest; do not dress too expensively or wear out-landish hairdos. We have seen pictures of women in other days who had their hair extended up for several feet with pearls and flowers and birds entwined in the concoction. Surely they must have had to sleep in a chair!

God says, "Show your faith by the way you live not by the way you dress."

Here again, we must not go to either extreme. We must not overdress or underdress. I have seen religions that order their women to wear long sleeves, tight collars, long dresses, no makeup, granny hairdos, black shoes, and no jewelry. Yet, the worthy women dressed in purple with God's approval.

BY LOOKING AT THEM

Do you remember the parable Jesus told about the man who had been possessed with a demon, and it was cast out (Matt. 12:43–45)? His house remained empty, and in time seven more demons came back with the first one. The moral of the lesson was that after his life was cleansed, and he was forgiven, he did not busily add substance.

He left his house empty, and in time an empty house fills up with emptiness. That is all the world has to offer. Add it all up, and its sum is nothingness.

The Christian is supposed to be able to give a reason for the hope that lies within him. To be able to give an answer means to know your Bible. To know your Bible is to fill your mind with fullness.

God is busy changing us, and He uses the Word to do it. So what is the result? We are daily changing and becoming like Him, and He is pure.

Our thoughts become as His thoughts and our ways as His ways. As it says in 1 Corinthians 2:13–16. By filling our minds with His Word, we become like Him, and our old life cannot move back in.

CHARACTERISTICS OF THE CHRIST-FILLED LIFE

Because we are in Him and He is growing in us, we can endure sufferings. "All who desire to live godly in Christ Jesus will be persecuted" (2 Tim. 3:12). God is always shaping us into better vessels for His use.

"We are always on the forge or the anvil; by trials God is shaping us for higher things" (Henry Ward Beecher).[39]

Suffering is a part of the plan. Do we think that only Christ should suffer? "Must Jesus bear the cross alone and all the world go free? No, there's a cross for everyone and there's a cross for me."

In time, we can even love our enemies. God never tells us to do something He won't help us to do. I can learn to make a decision to love my enemy before he has made the decision of his next plan to hurt me. Only can this happen to a life that is filled with His word,

As we grow, we will become fearless. God doesn't give us a fearful nature, "For God has not given us a spirit of cowardice, but a spirit of power and love and a sound mind" (2 Tim. 1:7). If God doesn't give us a cowardly spirit, then who does? Satan.

God tells women not to be fearful with their husbands—respectful, yes, but fearful, no. Many women are very fearful, but with God's instructions and His wisdom, they can overcome this nature.

By doing so, they will also please their husbands. Most husbands want a worthy companion but not a groveling one.

ᴔ A Holy Woman

This boggles our minds! How can we ever dare to think that we might be holy? I heard a preacher define holy by using another spelling, wholly. That makes it easier to aspire to. We want to be wholly committed to Him.

God taught in both the Old and New Testaments that He was going to make His children holy. "Because it is written, You shall be holy, for I am holy" (1 Pet. 1:16). What a job He has on His mind to take us, sinful as we are, and make us—holy. Or pure in heart. The Word still has the power to make us holy. Incredible as it may sound, we who are in training are becoming holy and pure!

Can We Be Pure?

Purity can only be achieved when we desire it, pray for it, and work at it. The desire for purity is a decision on our part. Training our minds not to dwell on unfit things is not easy when we are used to mentally pondering anything. It's work to concentrate on things lovely and honest and eliminate impure thoughts. But keep on working, girls; we must never give up.

It takes practice to kick Satan out of our minds. It takes work to look for pitfalls and possible dangers ahead. It takes discipline to take time to pray and to allow His Word in our minds. But that's how we become stronger and more able to recognize sin. We love the Lord more as we see Him working in our lives. Listen to the inspired mystery writer of Hebrews: "But solid food is for the mature, who because of practice have their senses trained to distinguish between good and evil" (Heb. 5:14).

Remember, all things are possible with the Lord. Our God is always with us, and as we beseech Him to help us, He hears us. Additionally, Jesus, our high priest, intercedes for us. God would never require something of us that would be impossible to attain.

> Therefore, since we have a great high priest who has passed through the heavens, Jesus the Son of God, let us hold fast our confession. For we do not have a high priest who cannot sympathize with our weaknesses, but One who has been tempted in all things as we are, yet without sin. Therefore let us draw near with confidence to the throne of grace, so that we may receive mercy and find grace to help in time of need (Heb. 4:14–16).

I don't know about you, but I sure do need mercy and grace all the time. Every day is a time of need for ol' Beck because Satan is after me constantly. But Satan cannot have me. I have promised my life, body, and soul to my Savior. Yes, I sin. But I am doing all that I can—constantly praying to God to help me walk with Him and live for Him. I start over. I ask for God to help me be pure and holy. I ask for forgiveness. And God forgives me constantly, because I am His. I ask for God's mercy. I cannot even begin to express how thankful I am for His unbelievable compassion and grace. I thank God for the following passage.

> Who is a God like You, who pardons iniquity and passes over the rebellious act of the remnant of His possession? He does not retain His anger forever, because He delights in unchanging love. He will again have compassion on us; He will tread our iniquities under foot. Yes, You will cast all their sins into the depths of the sea. (Mic. 7:18–19).

My passion is God. He is my everything, and I live for Him every day. I try with all my being to be on my toes when it comes to Satan and his attacks on my life, and then I always try to be on my knees, praying, because I desperately need my Father's help. I try to stand firm and convicted of God's power and love for me.

My desire is to be a 1 Corinthians 15:58 woman: "Be steadfast, immovable, always abounding in the work of the Lord." I want to have a clean slate with my Lord. This is the only way I know how to live, my sisters, I just want to live it right! I sometimes think I know exactly how David felt when he wrote in Psalm 16:8: "I have set the Lord continually before me; because He is at my right hand, I will not be shaken."

A WOMAN'S PRAYER

Our Father, we approach Your throne with so much love and thanksgiving in our hearts. You have taught us how to love through giving us Your Son, Jesus. With all our hearts we return to You this wondrous love. It is our prayer that we strive to be like Jesus, pure and holy. Please, Lord, forgive us, forgive us when we go astray and sin. Help us to guard our hearts and minds. We want to be like You. We love You and thank You for this life You have so kindly and mercifully handed to us. We are doing everything in our power to walk by faith and not by sight. We love You, Father. We love Jesus. We love the Holy Spirit. Thank you for being our God. In Jesus' name. Amen.

THOUGHT QUESTIONS

1. How do we become pure in heart?
2. How are prayer and purity connected?
3. What should we fill our minds and lives with?
4. How is it possible for us to be holy?

♪ **Song:** "Purer in Heart, O God, Help Me to Be"

Insights

It's All or Nothing at All

It's Friday morning, and I have a ton of things on my to-do list: clean the house, think about fixing supper, and write more about Titus 2. But instead I sat down with my breakfast and turned on the television to check my taped programs. Way back in the spring, I recorded parts of a miniseries called "The Bible." I began viewing it, and as with any biblical series, any student of the Bible can quickly see errors in Hollywood's version. If Hollywood would shoot a biblical movie the way it is written, it would be a blockbuster. However, the scenes of the Romans, Jewish life in Jerusalem, and life on the sea of Galilee were fairly well done, and I was compelled to watch more.

I am glad that I did. I hope I can express this the way it happened. As the story of Jesus unfolded—the calling of His apostles, walking on the sea of Galilee, teaching and feeding the multitudes—I was deeply touched by "Jesus." He was very real. He laughed; He touched the sick leper, and He was tender with the people—touching them, kissing them. What struck me the most was the way He would embrace them after He had healed their sicknesses! So sweet, so kind, so gentle.

I could not help but continue watching. Now, let me be perfectly honest and tell you that I never like to watch Jesus' crucifixion, and I have seen it depicted in many movies, with Mel Gibson's *The Passion of the Christ* being the most realistic. However, on this particular day, I was compelled to watch His suffering. I could not move from the couch.

The scourging is disturbing. The crown of thorns shoved on His head disturbing, but it is the crucifixion itself that is most disturbing. I forced myself to watch it, and I was brought to tears by the horribleness of it all, so unbelievably painful and cruel. I don't even have words to describe the driving of the nails into His hands and feet.

With absolute sorrow and agony, I watched as the Roman soldiers lifted up the cross and stabilized it in the rocky dirt outside of Jerusalem. I could feel the weight of Jesus' body as it hung there, suspended between heaven and earth. I could barely breathe; it was so real to me. He was beaten to a pulp; His back was bloody and torn; His face was bloody from being slapped, and the thorns of His crown, shoved so cruelly into His scalp, constantly dripped His precious blood. I cannot even imagine what any of this torture felt like—so brutal, so evil, so vicious, and so wrong. But remember, this was all part of God's plan.

> *What He asks us to do is nothing compared with what Jesus did for us.*

And all that I could think was: What is it, Lord, that You ask of me? What is it, Lord, that I can do to please You? What is it, Lord, that You want me to do? You want me to love my husband and children? I'll do it! Lord, You want me to be sensible and pure and kind? I'll do it! Lord, You want me to be a keeper at home and in submission to my husband? You've got it! As an older woman, You want me to be reverent, not a gossip, not enslaved to wine, and teaching what is good? I am there, Lord, I am there. I will absolutely do anything You ask of me. Anything.

Titus 2 is from the mouth of God, giving all ages the list of what God wants in us. So what is the big deal? This list pales in comparison to carrying an old, rugged cross and being cruelly nailed to it. Put the cross side by side with the qualities that God wants in an older man, older woman, young woman, and a young man, and there is no comparison. You see, obeying God in whatever He asks us to do is nothing when you compare it with what our Lord and Savior Jesus Christ has done for us. That old, rugged cross. The cross brings it home every time. In fact, the cross is home.

Life for the Christian bond-servant is summed up in these words: It's all or nothing at all. Remember that saying I have shared with you over and over? "A halfhearted Christian cannot serve a wholehearted Savior."

The primary reason I ever teach or write is because I love God, and I want to tell everyone I can about Him. I want to help you, the reader, to love God. I want you to see His magnificent love in sending Jesus to die for us.

Stand at the cross, my sister. Look at the Savior. Don't leave, just stand there at Calvary for a while. Take it in and absorb it down to your very soul. Look at the price that was paid for your salvation. Then there will be nothing you won't do for the Lord. There is nothing you won't change in your life for Him. There won't be any place you won't go for Him, and there won't be anyone you won't tell the Good News. Whatever God says, you will do. Whatever He asks, you will obey.

Yes, it is that simple. Why? Because the cross changes everything.

HOME
Sweet Home

"workers at home"

I do not have the words to describe how much I love the word *home*! It describes the place where my heart resides and loves the most in all the world. I have always been a homebody, and I can sure describe homesickness. Yes, God is number one in my life, and I live for Him. Next comes my husband and children and our dwelling place throughout the years—our home. It is my fervent desire to be that woman who Solomon described in Proverbs 14:1: "The wise woman builds her house."

Many times I have told my Jeff that I would live anywhere with him, even in a tepee, and that's just about the way our married life has been! We have lived in apartments, small houses, large houses, tiny duplexes, and large duplexes. I have come to this conclusion: It just doesn't matter, girls, where we live, as long as we live for the Lord. It is easy for men and us women to get wrapped up in the magnitude and magnificence of our mansion here on earth instead of the mansion that awaits us.

One of the saddest verses in the entire Bible is Luke 9:58 where Jesus told a disciple, "The foxes have holes and the birds of the air have nests, but the Son of Man has nowhere to lay His head." Jesus was the Son of God and a man on a mission: To save the lost. He had miles to travel, people to see, miracles to perform, and multitudes to teach. It is mind boggling to simply consider His daily tasks. But He had nowhere to lay His head. Few homes were open to the Prince of Peace who deserved the best bed and pillow the world could possibly offer. One can easily understand His falling asleep instantly on a boat and His frequent visits to Bethany where Mary, Martha, and Lazarus lived. Don't you feel that Martha had a room prepared for Him there? His home was in heaven, and that is the home for which He longed. As I write these words, I tell myself that the way Jesus lived is the way we should live—always teaching, doing, and being about our Father's business here; less emphasis on the luxury of the home that we do have and more emphasis on the home that is prepared for us in heaven.

PAUSE AND PONDER

Read John 14:1–3. What does this passage teach about Jesus' priorities?

Keepers at Home

It is time for us to jump into the pool again and see what the "take" is from other recognized religious authorities on being "keepers at home" (Tit. 2:5).

- *Albert Barnes:* "That is, characteristically attentive to their domestic concerns, or to their duties in their families . . . This does not mean, of course, that they are never to go abroad, but they are not to neglect their domestic affairs; they are not to be better known abroad than at home; they are not to omit their own duties and become "busy-bodies" in the concerns of others. Religion is the patron of the domestic virtues, and regards the appropriate duties in a family as those most intimately connected with its own progress in the world. It looks benignly on all which makes home a place of contentment, intelligence, and peace. It does not flourish when domestic duties are neglected; and whatever may be done abroad, or whatever self-denial and zeal in the cause of religion may be evinced there, or whatever call there may be for the labors of Christians there, or however much good may be actually done abroad, religion has gained nothing, on the whole, if, in order to secure these things, the duties of a wife and mother at home have been disregarded. Our first duty is at home, and all other duties will be well performed just in proportion as that is."[40]

❖ *Matthew Henry:* "Their business is to guide the house, give no occasion to the enemy to speak reproachfully."[41]

❖ *Adam Clarke:* "A woman who spends much time in visiting must neglect her family. The idleness, dirtiness, impudence, and profligacy of the children, will soon show how deeply criminal the mother was in rejecting the apostle's advice. Instead of . . . 'keepers of the house,' or 'keepers at home,' . . . several of the Itala have 'workers at home'; not only staying in the house and keeping the house, but working in the house. A woman may keep the house very closely, and yet do little in it for the support or comfort of the family."[42]

❖ *Wayne Jackson:* "Workers at home" (giving due attention to their husbands and children; the unjustified absence of mothers contributes to juvenile delinquency).[43]

What Do We Do?

Remember, we are keeping an open mind about God's Word here in Titus. Sometimes we disagree with God on a certain concept or topic, and His words are difficult for us to obey. We may have trouble with some of His teachings in the New Testament. What do we do? Do we just give up and refuse to conform to His will? Do we stubbornly demand our own opinion be heard? Or do we stop and pray about it? Do we ask God for wisdom and understanding to do His will even if we do not understand? What does a mature Christian do? She begs God for help!

I believe that my Father in heaven is in charge of my life. If He has commanded that I do specific deeds and actions, then I prayerfully do them because I have learned God knows what is best for me. I also know that God would never ask something of me and then refuse to help me achieve it. Above all things, God will bless me abundantly for being obedient. Whether I am the older woman approaching the younger woman with advice or I am the younger woman listening to the older woman, God wants both groups to have certain traits. Read Titus 2 again and ponder these attributes.

⟶⟫⟫⟩ **PAUSE AND PONDER** ⟨⟨⟨⟵

Read Titus 2:3–5 using KJV and NKJV. How is the phrase "workers at home" translated?

Fight God or Please God?

I learned a long time ago not to fight God. Do I want to repeat those times when I willfully sang the song, "My Way"? I absolutely do not! I have learned my lesson. If the Lord wants me to be a special kind of woman, then I will be that woman. I know that I am an older woman now, and hopefully I have acquired these seven qualities young woman should acquire. I may not have children in my home anymore, but I still have a husband to love, a marriage to be nurtured, and many younger women to teach.

If God's desire is for me to love my husband, love my children, and be sensible, pure, a worker at home, kind, and submissive, then His will be done! Why would I want to fight God? Being a Titus 2 woman is what I want too. Do you know why? Because more than anything else, I want to go to heaven. And going to heaven means pleasing God, which I love to do!

> *Choosing not to obey God results in absolute misery.*

These qualities that He desires to see in a woman's life are my goal now. I am not always kind, so I work on that. I need to be more submissive and not be a steamroller! So I back off and make sure that I am more in subjection to my husband, Jeff. If

God wants me to love my husband and children, then just watch me. I can work on that more. And if God wants me to be a keeper of my home, I will ask Him to guide me and bless me in that.

What I am trying to tell you, my sweet sisters, is that attitude is everything. I can make everyone miserable in my home, because if Mama ain't happy, ain't nobody happy! But if I am working on being loving and doing God's will, He certainly is there every step of the way. I have to admit that choosing not to obey God and work His plan results in absolute misery for me, for my husband, and for my children. I can either make my family happy in our home or I can make their lives miserable. Yes, we women and mothers have that kind of power. Audrey Hepburn once said, "I want my home to be a cheerful haven in this troubled world. I don't want my husband and children to come home and find a rattled woman. Our era is already rattled enough, isn't it?"

Just a Housewife

Let's sit at the feet of a wonderful older woman. Betty Bender has mentored at least two generations of God's daughters. Let's see what she has to say on the matter:

> Have you heard friends who are not attuned to God's teaching put others down by saying, "She is just a housewife?" Don't be intimidated by disapproval. Remember that this is the way the worldly "liberated woman" thinks. God's way is diametrically opposed to the worldly view. You are to be a representative of Christ in this task. Keep house as if He were physically present in your home. Feel complimented when others notice you are seeking to be at home with your family. If the truth were known, many women in the business world envy those who are able to be at home, giving their families the very best.
>
> Have other mothers made you feel like your children are underdeveloped if they aren't in nursery school? While nursery school can aid in developing our children, it is not a substitute, nor should it ever completely replace time at home under a mother's guidance.

Children miss so much when they don't have lots of personal care from their mother at home.

Have you been made to feel it is your responsibility to help your husband earn the living for the family? Because of the influence of the world, many husbands today expect their wives to bring in their share of the income. God's intended pattern is that the man should be the "hunter," the provider, and the wife should be the keeper at home. We function best in the roles for which God created us.

My heart cries for so many young mothers who are trying to balance a career and family. Both of these responsibilities are full-time jobs. No wonder they feel frazzled and tired most of the time. Sooner or later, they will be overwhelmed under the strain, or they will find that they are being neglectful in one of these two areas. Most often it is the family that suffers, because few employers will tolerate less than your best performance. It becomes worse than frustrating when you constantly have more to do than you can possibly accomplish. Many marriages are ruined and many children are lost to the Lord without either the husband or wife realizing just what went wrong. Or perhaps we just don't want to admit what's going wrong, for that would require dramatic changes in our lifestyle.[44]

MOM SAYS

God would not tell the older women to teach the younger women if there were not a natural desire to do the opposite.

There has probably not been a time in the history of man when women were so tempted to leave their homes and their children. Why?

1. to find "oneself"
2. to be thought ignorant and common if you choose to be only a housewife
3. to be accused even of being lazy if you stay at home

✆ WHOSE DOCTRINES ARE THESE?

There are women who want to stay home and are not permitted to. There are wives and mothers who must work to be able to survive. There are husbands who not only command that their wives work when it is not necessary but also covet their wives' income. There are temporary emergencies where a wife has to work, and there are those who work because they are bored at home and assign their responsibilities to others.

✆ WHAT DOES GOD SAY?

He says that the young women should be home with their children. Christians know this. We cannot expect the world to go against their nature, but we can expect the church to. The world lives in darkness, but Christians must be the light of the world.

Don't Christian young women get bored at home? Surely they often do. God did not say that the exception of the rule would be to those women who feel unchallenged at home and feel that they will go berserk if they have to change another diaper or mop another floor.

God looks at the end of the matter while we are overcome with the daily routine! He tries to show us that women are the hub of the family. Take the women out of the home and there will be chaos.

He does not write all the reasons for His commandments. He just says, "Stay home." Have you ever thought how large the Bible would have to be if God wrote out all the reasons for His rules? He gives us the positives, and time teaches us the negatives. Faith obeys, and our will rebels.

The heartbreaking truth of the matter is that when the children are grown or are in those difficult teenage years, the rut has already been furrowed. It takes daily living together to learn to know our children. We need to be the ones who hear their words and bind their wounds and give them quality and quantity time. We need to be there.

KEEPERS AT HOME

Many mothers are at home, but they are not a keeper of the home. The house and the children reflect our busyness or slothfulness. A mother propped up in front of the TV in her robe while the children are disassembling whatever is not a keeper of the home.

A mama in bed while her small children play can be guilty of criminal conduct. Would she pay a babysitter to do what she does? Children can get away from the best of mothers and be seriously injured or killed. It happens every day. Not only is the child destroyed but often the marriage is. The "what ifs" torture both parents. "If only I'd . . ." rings in their ears for the rest of their lives.

Many young mothers do not realize how quickly children can kill themselves! Children don't know enough not to drink poisonous things, not to play with scissors or knives, not to reach up and pull a pan of boiling liquid off the stove, not to play with matches, not to go into the street, and not to turn on the hot water while in the tub. (They are naturally drawn to water, and drownings occur quickly and frequently.) They seem prone to destruction.

BABYSITTERS AND PLAYSCHOOLS

More and more we are hearing about child abuse in these conditions. Not only are children being physically abused but also sexually. Most sexual deviates are the result of adults starting them on that way of life. And most of these adults were relatives or close family friends. The older women should be teaching the younger that it can happen to their children too. Children often do not tell their parents of these abuses. They have an instinctive shame.

One night we left our little boy with a teenage neighbor who had been begging to keep him. We left him asleep to just be gone for about two hours. When we came back, everything seemed normal, but our neighbor told us that the sitter had left the house after we did and only returned just before we came back. The house could have burned down in that time, or he could have awakened and cried and known that he was alone.

There are capable and dependable sitters and schools, but they cannot compete with the care of parents who love their children. There are times we need to be gone and to be away for relaxation, but do we need to be away forty hours a week?

THE MAN'S PUNISHMENT

After Adam sinned, God placed on him and mankind the making of a living for himself and his family as long as he lived. This was not placed on women. Her punishment was pain in childbirth. She is the weaker vessel, and God knows that she does not have the strength to do his work and hers!

I read the other day in a woman's magazine how little a man works at home. It was infinitesimally small—something like twenty-three minutes a day. Man believes that the home is the woman's responsibility. This article also said that the more the man helps at home, the more he resents having to.

So the working woman puts in her forty hours away from home and then has it all to do when she gets home. How long can she last physically, socially, and spiritually? Who pays the price for her weariness? The whole family and even God in her lack of service. There again, if she could only see the end of the situation, if she could know how it is to live with broken health and nerves, would she do it? No.

The things that shocked her at first no longer shock.

God told her that she was the weaker vessel and that she should be protected and be lived with in an understanding way. But she thought she was stronger than God knew.

History tells us that when our forefathers and foremothers moved here, the women could not survive those terrible winters. Most of them died before their time. I have seen those old burial grounds in New England. The man would be buried with several wives—wives who did not live long.

Now women are living seven to ten years longer than men, but it will be interesting to see if those statistics remain constant with the increase of the women working two jobs. (Seventy percent of married women with children who work have more heart attacks than those at home.)

ꙮ THE MARKET PLACE

God places women in the home. That is her arena, her palace. "Let our sons in their youth be as grown-up plants, and our daughters as corner pillars fashioned as for a palace" (Ps. 144:12). Pillars in a palace is God's wish for young women and older women too.

When a woman leaves the home to go into the marketplace, she is in the man's arena, the jungle. The sweat and the thistles become a part of her daily life, and it is sad to see her become a part of that carnal world. I read an article the other day teaching working women how to be executives. It taught her how to toughen up and secure and keep the best positions. The suggestions were given to help her overcome her femininity and to develop more masculine thinking.

She leaves her home as a protected Christian lady, and she goes out to hear the ribald conversations and suggestions. Many times she feels she has to bear the sexual overtures of her boss or fellow workers to keep her job. She is thrown with other women that she would not have been with at home, and she can quickly pick up their ways if she isn't careful. The things that shocked her at first no longer shock. In fact, she gets to where she can pretty well return what is thrown at her. To survive in the world, she becomes like the world.

A woman goes against her finer nature when she has to compete with the men in the world. She has to learn different ways, and those things she learns do not make for a better Christian home and a happier husband and children.

⁓ We're Picking Up the Men's Habits

Many women are now stopping by the bar for a drink before they go home just as the men have done for years. "Office wives" are becoming legion. A woman tends to confide more to a man she works with than the man she lives with. Women who are sent off to other cities get lonely and soon meet lonely men. "Everybody's doing it" will ever be a temptation, even to Christians.

It has been observed and proved that most men who make less than their wives cannot bear the competition. There is more wife beating and more profanity in homes where the wife is richer than her husband.

Women are more self-sufficient and are not trying to adjust to their husbands as they once did. It is much easier to leave their mates than to make a go of it. More and more women are leaving home. It used to be the man who walked out on his responsibilities, but now many women do too.

Women are often hiring people to take on their responsibilities. A working woman made the statement the other day, "What I need is a wife." She wants to come home to find a clean house, supper cooking, and the children looked after. So she hires it done instead of doing it herself.

She is expecting other mothers to bake the cookies, attend the PTA meetings, and babysit for her. "Will you pick up my children, take them to the doctor's office, check in on them at home, pick up a few needed groceries, or whatever?"

She also counts on other Christian women to do her part in the work of the Lord:

- ✤ "You'll have to bake the cake or bring a roast or whatever; I'll just buy some rolls and butter."

- ✤ "I can't be in on the workday—that's the only day I'm home, and I have to do all the things I left undone."

❖ "My work keeps me from attending the ladies' day and lectureships and learning sessions."

So our women do not have the time they once had for growing. Time is precious, and there is so little of it.

Many men feel justified in being an inactive part of the church because of their work. They feel they have the right—even the necessity—of getting out and exercising, because they are so tied down with their jobs. Working women are following their example.

Listen and think on this scripture:

> And the one on whom seed was sown among the thorns, this is the man who hears the word, and the worry of the world and the deceitfulness of wealth choke the word, and it becomes unfruitful (Matt. 13:22).

Not unfaithful but unfruitful.

✸ BE HOME LOVERS, NOT HOME LIKERS

It takes a long time to learn to be a home lover unless your mother taught you to be one. The worthy woman is our example. She made beautiful tapestries. She had time to be gracious and to live well.

Women do not have the time they once had for growing.

"She carried her food from afar." This brings to mind that her table was spread with not only ample food but a charming variety. She went to the trouble of feeding her household with delicacies. She had fresh fruits, fresh fish, and vegetables in season. She knew where and what to buy, and she had the time to do it.

Her meals were planned and not thrown together at the last moment. She put her good mind to the task of feeding her family well. God has given us a sound mind, and He hopes that we will learn to use it in our homes.

What are some practical ways we can learn to be a home lover? Magazines for women have lots of hints and helps and pictures and ideas. If you cannot afford to buy them, go to the library. Visit women with imagination and note stores that decorate beautifully. Swap ideas with other friends. This can inspire us to be more home conscious. Be imaginative. Let other women copy you!

When our husbands are pleased with our efforts, it encourages us to try harder. When we know that our merchandise is good, it gives us self-confidence and pleasure.

Garage sales have inexpensive little treasures that can be used to beautify our homes and our tables. It doesn't take a lot of money to produce a lovely home, but it does take imagination and time.

I remember a widow who moved to a little city where I lived. She had little or no furniture. She bought some unpainted chests and tables and second-hand furniture, and she painted it all red, white, and blue. It was absolutely striking. I used to bring people over to show them her house. She painted some chests white and then put red knobs on them and vice versa. She picked up cotton rag rugs in the right colors; she slip-covered the other furniture; she put the rest of us to shame with her originality. Anyone can spend money, but not everybody can make their place look beautiful and not spend much money. That is an art. Probably a learned one.

Hospitality is a command, and today that falls at the door of the women. Do we dare experiment with recipes? Do we pick up artificial flowers, old dishes, colored napkins, and beautiful records to play while we eat? Have we thought about putting a candle in a bottle with a candle ring of grapes, letting it drip down, a centerpiece for a spaghetti supper? Or paper flowers and Mexican ceramics for Mexican food? Or inexpensive Chinese figurines and little bowls for Chinese food?

I remember visiting some of my sweet Christian friends who have a lot more money than we do, and they had such beautiful homes. I noticed they had a lot of candles and grapes. I could not possibly compete with their lovely furniture, but I could afford some candles and grapes. (My husband says we have enough candles to heat the house for the winter.)

ENTERTAINMENT

What do you do after dinner? It is pleasant to just sit and visit. Some would rather do that. Others would enjoy games and we keep a lot of them on hand. Password, Dominoes (even double nines), silly card games like Spoons and Slap can be exciting and fun. We have found a game called the Ungame which is wonderful to play with families or new Christians or older ones. Now that we are getting older, it is more our speed. It has additional subjects to be discussed, and we have six different categories that we can play. All the trivia games can be fun—especially Bible Trivia.

If you are young and active, there is croquet, volleyball, and ping pong. They are great in getting to know each other. It is the being together that is important. Making homemade ice cream is always fun. And fattening.

These things take planning and energy. Someone has to be the pusher, and it probably won't be the woman who has worked all day or the woman who has a preschooler. It takes a strong body to do all the planning, cooking, and playing.

Many husbands will not be put out, but I have noticed that even though one might drag his feet and feel too weary to cooperate, in time he enjoys it. Just get the ball rolling and have the attitude that this is going to be great, and usually it will be contagious to the rest of the family.

I remember with nostalgia a place where we once live. There were six or eight families, all with young children. Someone would call and say, "Let's go to the lake." We had a regular menu of cut-up potatoes to fry, sliced tomatoes, fried Spam, ice tea, and a homemade cake from a mix. We would go out and fry the meat and potatoes and get all the food assembled while the men fished and the children hurt themselves. Then we would eat. Oh, those were the days, my friends. Inexpensive wonderful fun! Some of those children are now wives of deacons, preachers, and elders.

❧ A CLAIM OF GODLINESS

"But rather by means of good works as is proper for women *making a claim to godliness*" (1 Tim. 2:10).

How can we better make a claim for godliness? By having the home as our headquarters or with a job away from home? We are to be known for our good works, but it takes times to do good works. And energy.

It is a good work to be with our children, to keep our homes, and to love our husbands. These are all good works ordained by God.

We are not to leave our small children and homes to do good works. The time will come, anxious as we are to be out and doing, when we can more easily regulate Christian work outside our home. We will be able to service those in need and not neglect our priorities.

A dirty house and neglected children only cause the blasphemy of the world about the Christian wife. Instead of being a light, we may become an object of ridicule.

The church and the world know what our homes look like. God tells us to go and look and learn from the worthy women of Proverbs. He says, in effect, "Go and do likewise."

❧ HOW GREAT THE TEMPTATION

How great is the temptation to be away, to dress up each morning and be where the action is! How easy it is to lay down my burden of child raising and to pick up the lesser burden of working outside the home! How wonderful to have that extra income so I can dress better and furnish the house better. How boring to be at home! I would go crazy in a week! I hear this from women a lot.

Who is in this temptation business? "All these things I will give You, if You fall down and worship me" (Matt. 4:9). Satan never tells you about the end of the matter and what prices we pay for such homage. He knows better than that.

The alcoholic wishes he had never had that first drink; the smoker wishes she was not addicted; the worker away from the home is addicted too. "I've seen both worlds, and I'll take his" and "You can't stop me," they say.

You're right. The older woman can't stop you, but she has the responsibility to challenge you to try it God's way. She has the duty to tell you what God says to women, and then the choice is yours.

I gave these lessons in several lectureships and am getting responses from young women who say they have gone back home and are glad. I imagine I am going to get several letters that say, "Butt out." I won't live long enough to hear some of the same sisters say, "I wish I had done it God's way." We are all "too soon old and too late smart."

USING OUR HOMES FOR FINANCIAL BETTERMENT

The worthy woman did! She made girdles and sold them. She made them at home. The home can be a place to help the family out financially.

Godly women and men need to be training their daughters to be productive at home after they marry. Think about the occupations that can be done at home without the family being neglected. Babysitting, cooking, typing, tutoring, piano teaching, bookkeeping, and hair care. We should teach our sons to make a good adequate living for his family.

Look at the want ads and see the jobs that are advertised or people wanting someone to work at home. Handmade garments or crafts have taken America by storm, and that was what girdle-making was.

The working woman now seeks homemade goods, babysitters, dress makers, and house cleaners. She now can afford piano lessons. She can afford what the home-keeper can supply.

THE EMERGENCIES

If we are in a temporary financial disaster, the woman may have to help for a little while outside the home. Hopefully, this will never be. Somehow we always made it—even when my husband was out of work. God saw us through.

If you have to work, do it part-time if possible. Work while your husband is home with the children, if possible. Leave your small children with a Christian. Or better yet, leave your children with your own mother, though she probably didn't leave you.

Make your decision that you will put your money to the emergency, and do it! Make your decision that you will be back home as soon as possible, and be back home! Realize that God loves you and is concerned, and trust Him more and your own strength less.

Note as you work how much more it costs to work and how little you really can help financially. You have to have more gas for the car, often the second car. You cook differently—more expensive quicker meals, more eating out. You have to have more clothes; you have to pay the babysitter. You have a lot of extra expenses. Your income taxes go up. Also remember that you may become addicted, or your husband may become addicted for you to work. The kids will never be addicted to your being gone. Have you seen the TV commercial where the little girl begs her mother not to work, and the mother answers, "How can we buy your expensive designer jeans?" Or have you seen the insurance commercial that asks a grief-stricken husband and children, "How can you make it without her salary now that she is dead?"

ꙮ How Do We Get Our Husbands to See?

How do we get him to see that we need to be home? If he is a Christian, we show him Titus 2:3–5. We show him that we are unhappy in neglecting him and the children. We point out that our physical strength is limited. We help him to appreciate our wanting to have a clear conscience.

Really, we could point out the same things to a non-Christian husband. We work at having a clean house, good meals, and a happy home and show him the advantages of this. We are less tired and more loving, and hopefully he notes this as we stay home.

❦❧

Dear Meg,
I'm thirty-six and this is my second marriage. Pete's a wonderful man, terrific with my son and very helpful. We are in love.

So why am I writing? I just started working full time so we can buy our dream house. My job in a hospital is hard, physically demanding and very tiring because I work overtime.

There never seems to be enough time for us. We are rarely alone, and our love life has lost its sizzle. I'm too tired to make love the way we did before, so I just crash from exhaustion.

I'm crabby because I'm bone tired. We seem to be at each other's throats most of the time.

Any advice that you can offer would be appreciated.

—Bad Way, Baltimore, MD

❦❧

Dear Bad,
Fatigue can sabotage the best of relationships. Don't let it ruin yours. In your eagerness to buy that house, you are jeopardizing your health too. Please cut out the overtime. It will save your sanity as well as your relationship.

Exhaustion is no excuse for crabbiness or missed love-making, especially when it is self-inflicted.

—Meg

We need to pray for wisdom to learn to live within our means. Cut up the credit cards. Learn to budget. Learn to give to God, sacrificially, for He promises to turn around and give it back, pressed down and running over.

"Give, and it will be given to you. They will pour into your lap a good measure—pressed down, shaken together, and running over. For by your standard of measure it will be measured to you in return" (Luke 6:38).

HOW DOES HE FEEL?

Many older Christian women do not allow themselves to see the yearning in their husbands' faces as they leave the home for work.

Many men realize that their time is limited on this earth, and they want her to be with them as their own time allows. There is no pressing need for things now. But there is a dire need for each other.

A HOME LOVER

So when is the convenient time for the woman to leave her home? Never. Because "it takes a heap of living in a house to make it home" (Edgar A. Guest).

God appeals to us to be ever homesick for heaven. We are strangers and pilgrims here with temporary places of abode. He takes us from our "pleasant houses" to the home over there.

> By wisdom a house is built, and by understanding it is established; and by knowledge the rooms are filled with all precious and pleasant riches (Prov. 24:3–4).

> The Lord said, "In my Father's house are many dwelling places; if it were not so, I would have told you; for I go to prepare a place for you" (John 14:2).

The Lord says, "Come and see my home." When a woman loves her home, she, too, says, "Come, see my home, not my house, but my home."

The Lord Provides

How often we have heard William Wallace's words quoted: "The hand that rocks the cradle is the hand that rules the world." We women have untold influence and power over so many things and people.

I am most blessed in that when Jeff and I started our family, it was Jeff's desire for me to stay at home and be with our kiddos. I was so happy that he felt this way because that is what my heart wanted to do. We didn't have much; we lived in a very small house, but we had so much love there. We never did go hungry, as God provided all our needs. There would be times when we didn't know how in the world we would pay our bills, and there would be a check in the mail from the mortgage company or another whom we had overpaid. Interestingly enough, this check would always have a little more than what we needed. So when this happened, I always told my Jeff, "God must have wanted us to go out to eat!" I tell you, girls, God is more than good—He is fabulous! "Trust in the Lord with all your heart and do not lean on your own understanding" (Prov. 3:5).

But what I loved the most about being a keeper at home was simply being able to "be there." To hold my children, to love my children, to be there when they came home from school and tell them about God. I wanted more than anything else to raise my own children . . . and not entrust them to the lady down the street.

> I wanted more than anything else to raise my own children.

There is absolutely nothing more wonderful than rocking your child and teaching him about Jesus. How sweet it is to sing hymns with your children and to pray with them. I wanted to be the one to tell my children about God and His love in sending Jesus and the Holy Spirit to us. As they grew up, we had marvelous discussions about the church and its importance in our lives. Beholding my children being baptized were the two most monumental days of my life. Why? Because I saw that they loved God and wanted to do His will. My heart goes out to the many working mothers who are so exhausted they barely can get the food on the table. And where is the time for God? There simply is no time for Him. He takes a backseat in absolutely everything.

Listen to what David Lipscomb said about loving children:

> To love their children is to "nurture them in the chastening and admonition of the Lord" (Eph. 6:4 ASV). Love is the fulfilling of the law. Love to the child is to do what the law requires the mother to do for the child. Often mothers from a selfish feeling spoil their children. They deceive themselves, thinking it is from love. The Scriptures deal in practical questions, not mere sentiments. Solomon said: "He that spareth his rod hateth his son; but he that loveth him chasteneth him betimes" (Prov. 13:24 ASV). That is, he that fails to restrain his son and train him in the right way hates him. Many parents will be made to realize at the last day that they were the worst enemies of their children and had led them to ruin; that their mistaken and selfish feeling for them was hatred and not love.[45]

PAUSE AND PONDER

Name some important things a stay-at-home mom gets to do. Give at least two scriptures that she fulfills.

No Greater Career

I encourage young men to get the best job possible so that Mama can stay home when the babies start arriving. This is God's plan. Remember that He will help you when you are trying to be this woman of Titus 2. Trust in Him and pray for husbands to see. I saw this great quote on Facebook the other day and cannot find out who said it:

> Women can give up their jobs as clerks, engineers, doctors, etc., and other people will step in, and the world will go as smoothly as before . . . Not so with mothering. When we leave this job, the world does not go on as before. It falters and begins to lose its way.

Barclay said long ago, "In the last analysis there can be no greater career than that of homemaking. How many a man, who has set his mark upon the world, has been enabled to do so simply because someone at home loved him and tended him."[46]

Work Outside the Home

If you have to work, do everything possible to be able to take your child with you. School teaching is one of those jobs. Possibly your child can be with you at the same school. When I worked a while part-time, I substituted at my children's school only, and we went to school together and came home together. Recently, due to the COVID pandemic, many women are working at home.

> "There can be no greater career than that of homemaking."
> —Barclay

Please let me say this loudly and clearly: There are those who must work! There are no other options. The Lord is the only true and righteous judge of your situation, and the only one to whom you are accountable. Divorced, widowed, or unmarried moms are most often bread winners. There may be a time that you or I must return to the work force. Perhaps it was not part of the plan we had in mind, but these things do happen! Pray, pray, and pray some more to get back home. Ask the Father for help—He totally understands what you are trying to ask.

If you are locked into working and have children at home, please stop and reconsider. Your children need you. Don't fool yourself by saying "quality time" is what is needed in any family and not quantity time. That is not true. Our families just want time. Working in order to have the fabulous house, the fabulous furnishings, the fabulous vacations, cars, and boats often requires a stressful job with a sixty-hour work week. What price will you pay to escape the precious lives God has given you?

A dear friend of mine ran a small daycare out of her own home, taking care of a handful of children. She once expressed to me about one of the working mothers whose children she kept: "This woman does not make a lot of money at her job. In fact, her paycheck is spent on childcare. She doesn't care. She simply will not stay at home."

On the other hand, there is the mom who would give anything in the world to be at home, but she just cannot. My sweet sister, don't give up hope. Beg God for help. He is listening and He understands.

Always remember that your children will not be home forever, and you will be able to work later, if that is your desire. Enjoy your precious offspring and be sensible, smart, and wise about the time you have at home with your children, for when you turn around, they are already gone.

PAUSE AND PONDER

Research the song "Turn Around" by Dick and Dee Dee. How does this song relate to Psalm 39:4 and James 4:14?

TO THE MEN IN OUR LIVES

To our fathers, our brothers, and our husbands, too,
We have a request to make of you.
Would you learn to love us and let us be part
Of the dearest dreams you hold in your heart?

We live in a world of temptations galore—
To cheapen our bodies, our thoughts and more.
The custom of many is to leave their domain.
To leave their small children, a living to gain.

But God asked you men the living to make
And mothers be home for everyone's sake.
To love us, defend us, with the dragons to wrestle,
To remember, dear ones, we're the weaker vessel.

—Lea Fowler

⌐ A WOMAN'S PRAYER ⌐

Father, help us women to always want to do Your will. May our lives be a blessing to Your name, and may Jesus be glorified by our examples as mothers, wives, and workers. Please help us to truly love our homes more and to make the right decision for them that would please You. Please be proud of us—Your daughters. In Christ's name. Amen.

THOUGHT QUESTIONS

1. What is a home-lover?
2. Why is the lure of a career so attractive?
3. What do you do with a husband who pushes his wife to work away from home?

♪ **Song:** "Jesus Paid It All"

Insights

The Treasure

She came into my life when I was about five years old. Our family had moved from Odessa, Texas, to Marlow, Oklahoma, as my dad worked for Halliburton Oil Company in nearby Duncan. My mom went door knocking one day to see if anyone wanted to study the Bible. A lady named Nita Montgomery answered her door, heard Mother's question about studying the Bible, and said yes!

Let me back up right here and add that Nita was one of the sweetest, kindest, and most generous of women that ever walked the face of this earth. Blessed with beautiful brown eyes, it seemed that Nita possessed something my own mother didn't at the time: Nita understood me—she quickly became my second mama and also my champion.

It wasn't long before Nita obeyed the gospel, along with her husband, George. This sweet couple had three children—Leroy, Jerry, and Linda—about the same age as we Fowler children. The Montgomerys had a fourth child, Tammy, after we moved from Marlow. All of us kids found ourselves being thrown together quite a bit as our moms had instantly "hit it off" in the friendship department. That front door to the Montgomery home was always flying open and slamming shut with the antics of six lively children.

As our moms had found one another to be kindred spirits, Linda and I discovered we felt the same way. Thus, my first BFF (best friends forever) friendship came to be. We dressed a lot alike and had the same short page-boy-with-bangs hairdo. Linda had inherited her mom's kind brown eyes, by the way, and that hairdo looked heavenly on her. Me? Not so much. We spent hours making mud pies on our front porches, played "dress up" in our mothers' clothes, adored eating mayonnaise sandwiches and catching lightning bugs in jars on summer nights.

Linda and I were joined at the hip, and even now as I remember her face, I miss those glorious days of my youth with her. Our family moved away from Marlow when I was nine, headed to our adventure as missionaries in beautiful New England. Although Linda and I were separated, we were always joined in heart. I went on to college, and Linda married and had two precious children. She acquired more BFFs in her life and so did I.

Friends are the true treasures in this life.

So what are you getting at, ol' Beck? I am trying to tell you this: Friends are the true treasures in this life. And it is God who has so kindly given all of us this gift of friendship. Who can really describe the blessings of having a friend who understands and loves us no matter what? Rare is that friend. How do you describe the friend who is there through thick and thin and all the in-between moments, patiently listening for hours as we pour out our souls, our broken hearts, and our earnest desires, and vice versa? Do you understand what I am trying to say?

Not all friends are good friends or are even good for us. Beware. God knew that His children needed to be on their toes when it came to running with a clean crowd, so He inspired Paul to say these words: "Do not be deceived: 'Bad company corrupts good morals'" (1 Cor. 15:33).

Let's examine a few scriptures that express the beauty of friendship:

- ❖ "Oil and perfume make the heart glad, and the sweetness of a friend comes from his earnest counsel" (Prov. 27:9 ESV).

- ❖ "A friend loves at all times, and a brother is born for adversity" (Prov. 17:17).

- ❖ "A person of too many friends comes to ruin, but there is a friend who sticks closer than a brother" (Prov. 18:24).

Read all of Proverbs and you will find many references to the right kind of friends and the wrong kind too. God tells us of the good, the bad, and the ugly of relationships. He never sugarcoats the truth about people.

Is there a cost to friendship? Yes! The blunt truth of the matter is that friends require our time and our money. Friendship often requires us to counsel a buddy with a midnight crisis or suddenly make an unplanned trip to a friend's side who has just suffered a car wreck or to sit and listen and say nothing while a friend pours her heart out. Often there are no words we can say. The bottom line is that to have friends, one must be ready to make personal sacrifices. This requires work on our part—and physical stamina. Relationships require attention, strength, work—and above all things, prayer. No aspect of life escapes the need for God and His guidance.

Perhaps you want friends, but you are not quite sure how to begin. First, pray for God to lead you and pray to be like Jesus. Put a smile on your face and be friendly. Be warm, open up your arms and learn to hug people. Do this twenty-one times in a row. When something is repeated twenty-one times, it supposedly becomes a habit. Notice the children who cross your path. Hug them. They will learn to run and get their hug when they see you coming—even teens love hugs. You will be surprised how quickly you will learn to be friendly. People will be drawn to you, and you will be drawn to them. You can do this. The Lord will help you.

Don't you think it is important to love one another? Doesn't the Bible teach it over and over? John, the apostle of love, and was present when Jesus said, "This I command you, that you love one another" (John 15:17).

When we learn to love, we are being godly, for "God is love" (1 John 4:8). Embrace the older women and the younger women in your life. Develop and grow the relationships. Be loveable and pretty soon you will be a living and breathing Titus 2 woman.

A few years ago, my best friend Linda passed away. She had diabetes, suffered kidney failure, and slipped away from us all too soon. My heart broke when I heard that she had died. As I stood at her casket a few days later, my mind was filled with wonderful memories—all good and happy.

Sweet little Linda, I won't see you again this side of heaven, but I want to meet you at the gate, grab your hand, and go to your mansion—to your porch—and laugh and talk like we used to on earth. I want it to be like old times, to pick up where we left off, only this time will be better. God, Jesus, and the Holy Spirit will be there.

Just because our lives took different turns never meant that we stopped loving one another. That is what best friends do best—they never stop loving. We have an amazing and wonderful God who took two families and intertwined them into eternity. And all of this happened because one woman named Lea who loved God knocked on the door of another woman named Nita who needed God.

So long for a little while, precious Linda. And remember, you will always, always be my Treasure.

Be Precious Like
JESUS

"to be kind"

To be kind. Oh my, does that hit you like it hits me? Right smack dab in the face and heart! Who doesn't desire to be kind or to be known as a kind person or to be surrounded by kindness? We can all relate to this comment I once heard: "I'm so tired of people being ugly to each other."

Look at the opposite of kind—unkind. What is unkind? Right off the bat, what occurs to me is mean, hateful, rude, and merciless. Being kind is being merciful, compassionate, good, nice—and most of all—like Christ. And what is another term for Christlike? Christian. When you look up *kindness* in the dictionary, you should immediately see the word *Christian.*

Wayne Jackson defined *kind* as "good natured or considerate," stating that life was hard on the ancient woman, and there may have been great temptation to gruffness. Burton Coffman says of kindness: "This is one of the homely virtues that blesses mankind as much as any other."

The Greek word used here in Titus 2:5 is *agathos* which holds these meanings: excelling in any respect, distinguished, good, of a good constitution or nature.

The Father calls all of us to exhibit kindness. Paul was inspired to pen these words: "So, as those who have been chosen of God, holy and beloved, put on a heart of compassion, kindness, humility, gentleness, and patience" (Col. 3:12).

Who are the chosen of God? His children. Christians. You and us! The meaning of the words "put on" is in the sense of sinking into a garment. I like that. The Christian sinking into a heart of compassion, kindness, humility, gentleness, and patience. I can just picture us Christians wrapping up in these attributes like we do a warm robe.

> *By nature we are children of wrath (Eph. 2:1–3).*

A scene from *Anne of Green Gables* makes me think of gruffness. Matthew and Marilla are having an argument about allowing Anne, the orphan they have taken in, to attend a Christmas event. Matthew and Marilla are brother and sister, probably in their fifties. Neither have married nor raised children. It is the very early 1900s and Matthew says to Marilla, "There isn't any need for her to be raised as cheerless as we were, Marilla."

PAUSE AND PONDER

Who stands out in your mind as being kind to you as you grew up? What specific actions can you emulate to show the kindness commanded in Titus 2:5, Colossians 3:12, and Ephesians 4:32? How is it possible to view these verses as suggestions and not commands?

MOM SAYS

The little foster boy prayed thus, "Lord, help the bad people to be good, and the good people to be nice."

Why, oh why, is it so hard for Christian people to be kind? Why do we have to work at compassion, gentleness, a pleasant disposition, a friendly touch, and mercy? Shouldn't those qualities be natural now? Can't our time be spent rather on the study of the law, the plumbing of the mind of Christ, and the chewing of the meat of the Word?

Reason agrees. But study tells us that by nature we are children of wrath (Eph. 2:1–3).

It is natural to be "wrathy." It is natural to lose our tempers and be unkind. It is natural to say what we think in a certain tone and let the chips fall where they may. This spirit is still working in the disobedient, but we are not allowed the luxury of being unkind. We can't do what we please but what we must.

When you look back to a time you felt that you were justifiably right in blowing your cool and saying what you said, does it give you comfort now? Would you like to replay that scene with a different ending? I would.

TEMPER

When I have lost my temper, I have lost my reason too.
I am never proud of anything which angrily 1 do;
When I have talked in anger, and my checks were flaming red,
I have always uttered something I wish I had not said.
In anger I have never done a kindly deed or wise,
But many things for which I felt I should apologize.
In looking back across my life and all I have lost or made,
I do not recall one single time when my fury ever paid.

—Author Unknown[47]

We've all known people who were not even-tempered—always mad. Can a growing Christian be comfortable in sin? Of course not. Disobedience and unbelief are synonymous. What is the answer then? The hardest task in the world—dying to self. Becoming a new creature; crucifying the old person. God never commands us to do something He won't help us do.

This cannot be done without the help of the godhead. Paul said, "I die daily" (1 Cor. 15:31). It is a daily walk and a daily death. Unless we take up the cross daily, we cannot be His disciple (Luke 9:23). It gets down to the nitty-gritty, this walk with Him.

It is interesting where God put this instruction to be kind. He put it after telling us to be a home-lover and before commanding to be submissive to our husbands. There must be a connection. A kind woman's hospitable home often becomes an elder's hospitable home.

All Christians are taught to be kind. "Be ye kind one to another, tender hearted, forgiving one another, even as God for Christ's sake hath forgiven you" (Eph. 4:32 KJV).

> *"Gentleness will prevent many miscarriages in the born-again process."*

The world expects women—or used to expect women—to be soft spoken, easy to entreat, and nice. The world expects men to be aggressive and businesslike with both feet on the ground and a no-nonsense attitude. God expects His women and men to be kind like Jesus was.

Jesus continually showed us how to walk the new life when He was here on earth. He was never on the defensive. He knew what was in the hearts of men, but He loved them anyway.

He taught us to be as gentle as a dove. Too often we are as harmful as the snake! Matthew 10:16 says, "Behold, I send you out as sheep in the midst of wolves; so be shrewd as serpents and innocent as doves."

Our attitude toward the lost is, "I'll save you if it kills you." We need to leave the unsaved friend as a friend with the door open for future conversations. The world and the church have about as many problems as they can handle. The Christian has the problems and the solutions. Hopefully, as the world sees your ordered peaceful life, they are drawn toward you. My husband Russ says, "Gentleness will prevent many miscarriages in the born-again process." The truth has the power to convert the soul, but it needs to be in the hands of the kind. "The servant of the Lord must not strive," or "The Lord's bond-servant must not be quarrelsome, but be kind to all, able to teach, patient when wronged, with gentleness correcting those who are in opposition, if perhaps God may grant them repentance leading to the knowledge of the truth" (2 Tim. 2:24–25).

We must let the Word cut between the spirit and the soul, for it is that sharp. But the wielder of that sword must not cut. He must be gentle and kind.

JUDGMENTAL

Christians are often harder on other Christians than they are on the world. We talk and sing about how great it is going to be when we all get to heaven. But strangely, we have to work and pray to get along with each other in the kingdom on earth.

We are all stumbling along this narrow road, and a friendly helping hand would be welcome. We are children; we are sheep; we are young; we are terminal; and we don't know how to go out and come in. We are in need of mercy and compassion.

THE ALMOST CHRISTIAN

Broad is the way that leads to death,
And thousands walk together there;
But wisdom shows a narrow path,
With here and there a traveler.

—Isaac Watts[48]

God gives us the right to judge our brother's fruits but not his thoughts or motives. When we find ourselves criticizing our brother or sister, we should ask, "Are you taking the position that this one is lost and going to hell if the world ended today?" Most of us would back up and not go that far. Then if they are not lost and God approves of them, who are we to disapprove? Ouch! Surprise!

>>>> SURPRISE! <<<<

I dreamed death came the other night and heaven's
    gate swung wide;
With kindly grace an angel fair ushered me inside.
And there to my astonishment stood folks I'd known
    on earth—
Some I'd judged and labeled as "Unfit," "Of little
    worth."
Indignant words rose to my lips, but never were set
    free.
For every face showed stunned surprise, no one
    expected me!

—Author Unknown[49]

Somewhere I read this quote: "A young preacher spends the first ten to fifteen years preaching to the sinner, the next ten to the church, and the last part of his life concentrating on his own lack."

Kindness should come with age but does not always.

GETTING IN GOD'S WAY

Many women tend to help God out. The maternal and bossy spirit go hand in hand. We must be careful lest we become a meddler in other's business, though we feel our motive is right. God may say, "Lady, don't try to help Me. You'll only confuse yourself and slow down My process." We see this spirit in Peter at the transformation when he said, "Lord, let us build three tabernacles here." He tried to take over, but it was God's show.

None of us wants our faith to be questioned. Yet, it would be different if we only knew and believed that God knows about the situation, is working on it, and will change it if it needs to be changed!

If in "casting our cares on Him" we can let go and let God, it will spare us a lot of worry and unkindness.

God is not a hard task master, but too often we are! God gives justice and mercy. If we are not careful, we will ask justice for the brethren and mercy for ourselves.

A lady psychologist remarked in one of her books that we need to remember that most of the world is only three years old. How much kinder we would all be if we treated each other as we would treat the toddlers or as we treat our pets. Personally, I'll take any kindness that comes my way. I need it.

THE MOST DIFFICULT KINDNESS

Hospitality is a hard saying and an almost forgotten art with the majority of Christian women. It doesn't come easy. There are a few in each congregation who open their homes, very few.

God's highest list for men to aspire to is the qualifications of elders. To be an elder he must have a hospitable nature. Now a man can be just about as hospitable as his wife lets him be. Who goes back the second time to a cold hostess? But he has to learn along with his wife and children the price of hospitality.

It is like the art of learning to give. It is giving. It takes time before it is a pleasure. In Old Testament times, the men were avid hosts. They felt the responsibility of entertaining and protecting their guests. Abraham fed the angels, and Sarah eavesdropped in the tent. Eavesdropping is easier than entertaining, and sometimes more interesting.

> *There is no way to learn to love each other more than by eating together!*

Today hospitality falls upon the woman. It is her job to clean the house, buy and prepare the food, entertain the guests, and do the cleanup afterward. Yet God reminds her husband that she is the weaker vessel.

God says the husband must take the lead. And how it helps if he will! The most hospitable home I was ever in was one of an elder who was an example to other men. When we think back about visiting his home, we think of his graciousness. He met us at the door. He seated us. He fixed the barbecue. He saw that our plates were kept full. He ate last. He kept the conversation going, and he made us feel like we were extra special to him. I still think we were.

I believe that more women would want to be more hospitable if their husbands would take the lead. It is hard for the hostess to keep the conversation going when the men won't talk. She is afraid that she will be labeled empty-headed and a chatterbox if she continues to try to keep the conversational ball rolling alone.

THE SHARING OF OUR HOMES

Our homes are our castles, our hiding places, our bulwarks, our havens, the place where we are the most vulnerable. Visitors see the cobwebs, the dust, the mice droppings, the mistakes, and many other undones of our lives. I remember going to a friend's house too early one morning, unexpected. She peeked through the door with her hair in rollers and was still in her bathrobe. "Oh, it's you. You can come in." Which meant if it were anyone else, she would bolt the door. A dubious compliment but one I understood.

Guests see the tension of the home. They see the lack of cooperation between the husband and wife, if it is there. They see the discipline or lack of it with the children. They see the emphasis of the setting of the table and the quantity and quality of the food. They see us!

And yet, paradox that it is, they also see the love and humor and fun and quality of that home, if it is there. There is no way to learn to love each other more than by eating together! The early church spent a lot of time eating together from house to house.

God put one of the greatest heartbreaking sentences on the one who was withdrawn from when he said, "You can no longer eat together." That would not be a hard sentence today, for the disciplined brother would say, "I'm not going to miss what I've never had."

ᴛᴇᴀᴄʜɪɴɢꜱ

"Be hospitable to one another, without complaint" (1 Pet. 4:9). Have an open-house feeling in your heart, for when the need arises or just for fun.

We have an example in Proverbs of a selfish man's hospitality:

> Do not eat the bread of a selfish man, or desire his delicacies; for as he thinks within himself so he is. He says to you, "Eat and drink!" But his heart is not with you. You will vomit up the morsel you have eaten, and waste your compliments (Prov. 23:6–8).

It is uncomfortable to be the victim of forced hospitality.

> If the house is worthy, give it your blessing of peace. But if it is not worthy, take back your blessing of peace. Whoever does not receive you, nor heed your words, as you go out of that house or that city, shake the dust off of your feet (Matt. 10:12–14).

Would our house be chosen? Would we welcome the stranger with no baggage? Would he stand outside our door and shake his feet so God could see that he knew that he was not welcome during his stay?

> Let love be without hypocrisy. Abhor what is evil; cling to what is good. Be devoted to one another in brotherly love, give preference to one another in honor; not lagging behind in diligence, fervent in spirit, serving the Lord; rejoicing in hope, persevering in tribulation, devoted to prayer, contributing to the needs of the saints, practicing hospitality (Rom. 12:9–13).

Practice hospitality. Practice makes perfect. There is a lot we can learn about sharing our homes and tables with practice. One of the hardest lessons I had to learn was to be moderate in my serving. If a large family came for a few days. I cooked a turkey and a ham and all the in-betweens that go with those, cakes and cobblers and other goodies. I couldn't do less with a clear conscience. I can now. Occasionally! I learned what it does to me emotionally. It sets me in the frame of overdoing and frustration before the company ever arrives.

Maybe we get more influenced by the term "entertaining" than by hospitality. I have been long on entertaining and short on hospitality. The elder who was so hospitable did not seek to entertain us. He just served us and loved us. Practice may teach us that.

Have people in because of the kindness of your heart, and be kind to them while they are there. And leave a kind feeling between you as you part.

You know He wouldn't have to teach us so much about this art if it were not a difficult assignment. There is very little, if any, teaching on being available for a dinner invitation. That is one of those things that comes naturally!

> *One of the hardest lessons I had to learn was to be moderate in my serving.*

It is my conviction if we would restore this lost art and open our hearts and our homes to those who need us, that the church would again be the leading religious group of America! Women are so important in God's plan of redemption. He meant for them to have the time and inclination to be known for good works. There is no better work than this, for it leads not only to conversations but to a strengthening of the brotherhood—and an agape love for each guest.

"Choose you this day whom ye will serve . . . but as for me and my house, we will serve Jehovah" (Josh. 24:15 ASV). And tables. It's easier than footwashing! Or maybe God counts it as footwashing!

⟲ Don't Make the In-laws Outlaws

Men are told to leave their parents and cleave to their wives. Women usually cleave to their parents.

The children know their mother's parents best because Mother goes home as much as possible. Kindness teaches us that our husbands want to go home too. His parents yearn for their grandchildren as much as her parents do.

Can we learn to be fair? Can we stifle our own selfishness? Will we conscientiously endeavor to do better from now on?

> "When we are born into an earthly family, we're given the spirit of man; when we're born into the spiritual family, we're given the Spirit of God"—Anonymous.

One section of the fruit of the Spirit is kindness. Goodness is another. Gentleness—another. "Against such things there is no law."

Remember, your son will marry someday, and you will be a mother-in-law!

⟲ Follow after Peace

"Pursue peace with all men, and the sanctification without which no one will see the Lord" (Heb. 12:14). Other translations give clarification and confirmation to this passage.

- ✤ "Always be wanting peace" (Jerusalem Bible).
- ✤ "Aim at peace" (NEB).
- ✤ "Let it be your ambition to live at peace" (Phillips).
- ✤ "Strive for peace" (ESV).

The mood of the woman usually permeates through the house and is catching. There is going to be discord in the best of homes. How blessed is the home where the mother follows "after the things that make for peace" (Rom. 14:19 KJV).

God has given to women this job: the pleasure of setting the stage, the home of comfort and sensual beauty, and the sound of peace.

How good He is to us women! How necessary godly women are in His plan for order and harmony! How blessed the homes of worthy women!

Are we known as kind, hospitable women?

A WOMAN'S PRAYER

O my Father, how kind You are to me! I bow before Your royal throne and praise Your holy name. No one loves me like You do. Father, I love You with all my heart and I thank You for Your kindness, Your mercy, and Your compassion. Help me to have the same kindness, mercy, and compassion You do. You have suffered long with me and my weaknesses and my lack of faith. Please don't ever stop loving me. I need You so. In Jesus' name I pray. Amen.

THOUGHT QUESTIONS

1. Why are Christians harder on each other than they are on the world? List one specific way to prevent this attitude.
2. Why is hospitality a difficult kindness?
3. Name some ways we can "follow after the things that make for peace."
4. What actions are opposite to kindness?

♪ Song: Angry Words

I have chosen the song "Angry Words," written in 1867, for you to sing as you close these thoughts. We all know this song by heart, but I really hope that you will sing the verse—the last verse—which is written by a mentor of mine, Betty Bender. She wrote the third verse in 1992, and it says so much about being kind. To me, it's the icing on the cake for this chapter.

> Let our words be sweetly spoken
> Let kind thoughts be greatly stirred;
> Show our love to one another
> With abundance of kind words.
>
> "Love one another," thus saith the Savior;
> "Children, obey the Father's blest command;
> "Love one another," thus saith the Savior;
> "Children obey the blest command."

Becky and her mom with new baby Jennifer, 1975

Insights

Biscuits and Grits

This morning was my morning to do something nice for my Jeff. Now I don't deliberately dedicate a day to him, but our Saturday began as a regular Saturday. We love to have a big breakfast. We were not going to do anything extraordinary this particular day, but when he left to do an errand before breakfast, something crossed my mind.

I had gone to the freezer to get out those Walmart frozen biscuits—which we love. They are easy-peasy. Well, there were no biscuits. Oh no! There is always toast, but I really don't want toast. I want biscuits. I groaned for a moment as I realized I would have to make them. Groan, groan, and more groaning. But Jeff loves my homemade biscuits. It's the one thing I asked my mom to teach me before I walked down the aisle! And man, can I make biscuits now! I screeched to a mental halt, thinking about all these riveting, exciting "husband" thoughts I had been laying on you precious girls in the writing of this book, and thought to myself, "Well, ol' Beck, don't you think you could 'love your husband' this morning?"

So I went to work. I whipped up those Fowler biscuits and decided that man of mine would get another treat from me—grits! Not instant grits. Never instant grits. But quick grits cooked slowly, beaten to death, and buttered—a delicious delight for the North Carolina boy I married. They are a mess to cook, but my man is worth it. I could hardly wait until he returned from his errand.

Jeff walked in from the garage and instantly noticed me standing there, stirring the grits. He never misses a thing. He looked at me surprisingly and questioned, "Grits?" I said to him, "Come closer." He came to my side, and I slowly opened up the oven door where he could observe the beautiful, lightly browned, exquisitely rounded, gourmet—did I say beautiful—Fowler biscuits sitting there so smug and so fine on a forty-eight-year-old dented pizza pan.

How could I have missed such an opportunity to learn and to grow?

He didn't say a word. He just grabbed me and hugged me—a nice, long hug. My heart soared to the highest heaven. Now, girls, that's lovin' your man. Being submissive to him? No problem. Why? Because it always feels good to do the right thing. And when you do what is right, when you obey God, you are Sarah's child. And never forget: God. Loved. Sarah. And God. Loves. You.

As you read the next chapter, you will understand.

CHAPTER 9

The BUCK Stops Where?

"being subject to their own husbands"

As I write this morning, I have these thoughts about this Titus 2 woman. What strikes me is that she is a good woman. She is also a kind woman. She loves her husband; she loves her children; she is sensible; she is pure; she is busy at home; and she is in subjection to her husband.

It Begins and Ends With . . .

As already mentioned, the seven qualities God wants in a younger woman begins with her husband and ends with her husband: "so that they may encourage the young women to love their husbands, to love their children, to be sensible, pure, workers at home, kind, being subject to their own husbands" (Tit. 2:4–5).

He is her "bookends." As my sweet sister Peggy says, "Any point neglected is detrimental to 'loving your husband.' " Some younger woman may say, "Well, I do not have a husband, so these qualities do not apply to me." Not so fast, my sister.

God has a plan for us all (Jer. 29:11–13). No one escapes. He is omniscient, omnipresent, and omnipotent—He knows all, is everywhere, and is all powerful. He knows all about you and me, from the tops of our heads, to the bottoms of our feet, all the in-between and especially all that goes on in our minds. Everything. Perhaps you have no husband; perhaps you are a widow; perhaps you are divorced; perhaps you have never married. What is God telling you?

First of all, take the qualities that do apply to you. Do you have children? Love them. How absolutely imperative that Christian women be sensible; be pure; and be kind so that God's precious Word will not be mocked or blasphemed! Not mocking God's Word is everyone's goal to begin with. Just because there is no man in a woman's life currently does not mean that she is excused from being a Titus 2 woman.

God Is Calling

Remember the older woman? Let's not forget about her either. This passage from Titus gives both sexes God's instructions and it covers all ages. When you and I were younger, hopefully an older woman loved us and guided us in the seven traits God prescribed in Titus 2.

What if no older woman had stepped up to the plate to mentor me and help me spiritually? What was I supposed to do with the "magnificent seven"? I am still called to love my husband, love my children, be sensible, be pure, be a worker at home, be kind, and be submissive to my husband no matter what comes my way. The list God has given to women—young and old—is not conditional. God has not given us a list of suggestions, my sisters. These are genuine commands. And this list will always stand as a herald and a beacon—God's calling to His daughters. All these qualities must become part of the fabric that God designed for us to be as Christian women.

Our Lives Are but Puffs of Steam

Those years as a young woman, constantly running with husband and family, flew by. When I was in those years, I had little concept of time. One day I looked in the mirror and saw my mother's face. What a shock! I had become the older woman somehow. I didn't feel any different, but my circumstances had definitely changed. My precious children grew up, left home, pursued college degrees, and married. You older girls know what I am talking about.

Now I am older and more mature in the faith. As God's child, I can help the younger woman acquire the characteristics God expects of her. I am here to help her. But I must make absolutely sure that I have the four qualities God expects of me. I must not be irreverent, or a gossip, or a drunkard, or a false teacher. All of these directives take lots of work. When you really think about it, the older woman has eleven qualities God wants her to possess—the seven she was to acquire as a young woman and now four more as an older one. Wouldn't you say that the older woman has the biggest responsibilities of all? You know, that just scares me to death!

You see, whether I have a husband or not, these verses still apply to me. In other words, you cannot run and you cannot hide from God's Word. It hits everybody just the way He planned.

Being Submissive

To some women, *submissive* or *submission* is a vulgar word, a word they refuse to use because they are not in submission to anyone, anything, or anybody. It simply is not in their vocabulary. Forget it. But God still says it.

> Older women likewise are to be reverent in their behavior, not malicious gossips nor enslaved to much wine, teaching what is good, so that they may encourage the young women to love their husbands, to love their children, to be sensible, pure, workers at home, kind,

being subject to their own husbands, [emphasis mine] so that the word of God will not be dishonored (Tit. 2:3–5).

Just so that everyone has a clear understanding of submission, let's see what the dictionary says: "The action or fact of accepting or yielding to a superior force or to the will or authority of another person."

In everyday language, submission is yielding oneself to the authority of another. Someone else is in charge, the boss, and you and I must yield willingly to this person. In the case of husband and wife, God tells wives to be submissive to their husbands. Let him be the boss, girls, and have the final say.

Does this mean that a husband and wife cannot discuss issues and make decisions together? Absolutely not. That is what couples do, for the most part. However, the final decision in a marriage is to be made by the husband, whether it is a wise decision or not and whether the wife likes it or not. Is this easy? No.

Personally, I do not want to make all the decisions. I have enough on my plate without making the final decisions for my family. God has put the man in charge and submission to the husband pleases God.

If a husband and wife have problems in this area, the answer is always to pray, pray, pray. God will help.

Examples

Submission is not a new concept. Let's look at some other passages in the Bible concerning subjection or submission.

> In the same way, you wives, be submissive to your own husbands so that even if any of them are disobedient to the word, they may be won without a word by the behavior of their wives, as they observe your chaste and respectful behavior. Your adornment must not be merely external—braiding the hair, and wearing gold jewelry, or putting on dresses; but let it be the hidden person of the heart, with the imperishable quality of a gentle and quiet spirit, which is precious in the sight of God. For in this way in former times the holy women

also, who hoped in God, used to adorn themselves, being submissive to their own husbands; just as Sarah obeyed Abraham, calling him lord, and you have become her children if you do what is right without being frightened by any fear. You husbands in the same way, live with *your wives* in an understanding way, as with someone weaker, since she is a woman; and show her honor as a fellow heir of the grace of life, so that your prayers will not be hindered (1 Pet. 3:1–7).

Let's break down 1 Peter 3:1–7:

- Submission without a word, by behavior only (v. 1).
- Internal adornment, not external (vv. 3–4).
- Sarah obeyed Abraham and was in subjection to him (vv. 5–6).
- A husband is to understand that his wife does not have the strength he does, but husband and wife are equal in inheriting salvation (v. 7).

PAUSE AND PONDER

Read 1 Peter 3:1–7 again. How powerful is submission in winning souls? What two words describe the behavior of a submissive wife? What is her focus? What word describes how God sees her?

In Submission

In 1 Peter 3:1–7 we see that in the Old Testament there were holy women who loved God, were adorned with good hearts and gentle spirits, and were submissive to their husbands. I think of Rebekah, Ruth, Naomi, and Esther. Peter then is inspired by God to mention that Sarah obeyed her husband Abraham, and even called him "lord" which means master. Sarah and Abraham were half-brother and half-sister. She had known him from her childhood, and yet, here she is put before us women as a wonderful example of submission. God wants us to notice her! We know from reading the book of Genesis that when Sarah overstepped her boundaries and tried to assist God in producing an heir for Abraham, she made a royal mess. She should have been more patient with God and His time instead of taking things into her own hands. However, God still loved her and honored her by naming her in the Hebrews Hall of Fame (Heb. 11), and He once again honored her here in 1 Peter 3, holding her up as an example of what a wife should do.

The last sentence of 1 Peter 3:6 tells us women that we are Sarah's children if we do what is right and not be fearful. Have you ever noticed this passage before? Remember, Sarah only had one child, Isaac. However, our Father bestows upon her more children—daughters she never had in real life. What was Peter trying to tell Christians here? He was emphasizing the need for all Christian women to obey God like Sarah obeyed Abraham.

When was the last time you and I were called "Sarah's child"? We women would be so foolish not to love her, obey like her, and be submissive like her. I can tell from reading about her that God certainly loved her.

Notice three verses from Ephesians apply here.

Wives, be subject to your own husbands, as to the Lord. For the husband is the head of the wife, as Christ also is the head of the church, He Himself being the Savior of the body. But as the church is subject to Christ, so also the wives ought to be to their husbands in everything (Eph. 5:22–24).

Note that wives are to be in submission to their husbands just like wives are in subjection to Jesus. If we are having a problem with being in subjection to our husbands, we need to understand that the very same subjection applies to us surrendering to whatever Christ commands.

In Everything

There is a zinger in Ephesians 5:24, and if you know me, you know I love zingers. (Zingers are statements made by God that we don't always notice, and sometimes they jump right off the page!) Look at the little phrase: *in everything.* We know that the wife is supposed to be in subjection to her husband, but in case we didn't get the entire picture, God adds the words "in everything." God knows us women. He knows how our minds work because He created them. So He spells out the details here. He knows that some daughter, somewhere, will say, "Well, I am in subjection to my husband. I do what he says. I let him handle the checkbook and make most of the decisions. That's enough." But that's not enough. That is not being in subjection to our husbands "in everything."

> But I want you to understand that Christ is the head of every man, and the man is the head of a woman, and God is the head of Christ (1 Cor. 11:3).

Oh, how I love this scripture, don't you? We are *all* under subjection to someone . . . even Jesus is! Paul appeals to the church at Corinth to understand this concept, and God, through Paul, appeals to all of us to understand this hierarchy too. There is an order of authority and it goes like this: Woman, man, Christ, and God. Believe me, I love being at the bottom of that totem pole!

Weaker and Yet Equal

There is one more point that God wants men and women to notice.

> You husbands in the same way, live with your wives in an understanding way, as with someone weaker, since she is a woman; and show her honor as a fellow heir of the grace of life, so that your prayers will not be hindered (1 Pet. 3:7).

Women are the weaker vessels when compared to men. I once asked my mom what this scripture meant. I recall her saying something like this, "Well, I think it means that women do not have the strength physically men have. She can't lift a couch, but he sure can!" Let's also notice that men and women are both heirs of the grace of life. Here men and women are both equalized when it comes to salvation. God sees no distinction when it comes to souls of men and women. We are equal and the same. Let's be women of God, as one author expressed on Facebook:

Women of God can never be like women of the world.
The world has enough women who are tough, we need
    more women who are tender.
There are enough women who are coarse, we need
    women who are kind. There are enough women
    who are rude, we need women who are refined.
There enough women of fame and fortune; we need
    women of faith.
We have enough greed; we need more goodness.
We have enough vanity; we need more virtue.
We have enough popularity; we need more purity.

—Margaret Nadauld

More Teaching from Betty Bender

God intended marriage to be a powerful union to accomplish great things that one alone cannot accomplish. We can destroy that power by disregarding the role that we are supposed to fill. Both the husband and wife must remember that the instructions in Ephesians 5:22–33 are preceded by instructions to all Christians to "submit to one another out of reverence for Christ" (Eph. 5:21 ESV). Both husbands and wives should respect their spouse enough to submit to the other so that they can work together for the family. We should all work together in our marriage for each partner to have the freedom to function fully, using all of our talents for the common cause of developing the best family possible. This will bring us fulfillment and happiness and glorify God.

If a young woman goes into marriage understanding her role as a helpmeet —one essential to help her husband become a more complete person—then she will see that she has a God-given, highly elevated, respected position and will endeavor to fill it as God intended. She will realize that by taking on the obligations and privileges of marriage, she has chosen to be in submission to her husband.

As we live side by side with those in the world, it is easy for us to forget that we belong to God, and we must look to Him in all things for our direction. Satan is extremely crafty and often brings

talk and concepts to our ears that we need to examine closely before we accept them into our minds as something we should follow. He proclaims a different doctrine that is diametrically opposed to God's Word. We cannot follow both but must choose whom we will follow.[50]

MOM SAYS

God is so wise. Note His order in this instruction to the teaching of the young women. Teach them first to love their husbands, and then to love their children. At the end of the list, He says for them to learn to be submissive to those husbands.

God doesn't put this at the beginning of the instructions but at the end. And just before He gives this teaching, He puts in kindness.

Husbands, all husbands, yearn for kindness, peace, and a woman who will adapt to his lead. Do you remember the survey we quoted where men put compatibility at the head of their list of "wants"? In essence, a man's desire: "I want a woman I can get along with most of all."

THE MARKETPLACE

He spends most of his working time away from home. His thoughts are bought by his employer, also his energy and his youth. His body needs rest and replenishing at the end of the day. His soul needs rest, too, and peace, love, and understanding. He marries and takes a wife for life, "in sickness or in health, for richer or poorer, till death do us part." That is a contract made by two adults.

Though he leaves the marketplace for his home, the world still presses in on the family. The desire for luxuries is ever present. The strife of discord lurks, and the TV brings in its suggestions for what the world thinks it needs.

If we are not attuned to the Word of God and if our eyes are not looking toward the only light there is, our reflective light may flicker and die.

‿ⁿ BEING SUBJECT TO THEIR OWN HUSBANDS

In God's instructions to the older women of what to teach the younger women, He begins with loving their husbands. Now the list circles back to the relationship between the husband and the wife. God stresses the importance of this tie, for the husband is the encircler. We must remember all the in-between instructions, such as being sensible, loving the children, being kind, chaste, and discreet. But the beginning thought is to love our husbands, and the ending thought is to adapt to them. To encourage their lead.

Let's consider some of the other versions and see if we can pick up any fresh thoughts on Titus 2:5:

- ✤ "Being in subjection to their own husbands" (ASV).

- ✤ "Obedient to their own husbands" (KJV)

- ✤ "Willing to adapt themselves to their husbands" (J. B. Phillips).

- ✤ "Submissive to their husbands" (RSV).

It used to be in the marriage ceremony the bride was asked to say that she would obey her husband. I don't think this is included in the vows anymore. It has become old-fashioned and archaic to feel that women are expected to be obedient any longer.

What does God say? He wants us to have a loving happy home. It is a credit to Him when we can show the world that Christianity produces happiness. He is spelling out to the younger women that the home will be happier for them if they are gentle and kind and obedient to their husbands. It takes faith to believe it, but it is so!

What would you give for peace? Its price is above rubies! There has to be a place "where the buck stops," a place for the final decision. God says the man is to take the lead and the woman is to follow.

All men won't lead and all women won't follow, but the ideal is for the man to diligently take the oversight of his household. The ideal is for the captain to sail his ship with order and discipline. The ideal is for the president of the company to know his workers and to superintend his plant and to make it a success. When failures come, the responsibility goes back to the head of the establishment, not the crew.

Many foolish women tear down their own houses. "The wise woman builds her house but the foolish tears it down with her own hands" (Prov. 14:1). We are in the generation that will go down historically as the time of the disintegration of the homes of America.

The mothers are gone; the children are on drugs, and the husbands are in shock! What happened? Is there any way to turn the tide back? Can order be restored? In the world, probably not. In the church, we have the answers in the Word of God, but do we have the faith? Or inclination? Is it working out? No. Aren't women to be their husband's helpers? Yes. What if a man cannot support his household without the help of his wife? Let's go back and look at the worthy woman one more time.

Did she help her husband financially? Yes. Did she leave the home to do it? No. She made girdles and sold them. (A lot is said about how much she sewed. Evidently, that was her talent.)

There are many talents (mentioned previously) that we can use at home that can be a lot of help financially to our husbands. We mothers need to see that our daughters develop ways of helping financially. Tutoring, piano lessons, typing, bookkeeping, baking, sewing, craft making, and many other various talents can be honed and perfected and used if necessary. And yet the "hub" is home.

❧ THE PRICE

Most Christian women admire a gentle, kind, and obedient wife and wish that they were more like her. We can all write a list of names of women who seem to naturally have the sweetness and submissive spirit that is to be yearned for.

How we note the young people who are polite and pleasant and show the training of a good home! We want to raise that sort of young people. We want to have a loving relationship with our husbands and to raise marvelous children. Don't we?

This is why we need to take to heart this teaching in Titus, for it is the recipe for a happy home. It can be ours if we read, work, and pray to that end.

I remember the story of a famous pianist who played at a concert. A fan rushed up and said, "I would give the world to be able to play like that!" The pianist answered, "No, you wouldn't because you wouldn't practice the hours a day that it takes."

The moral to that story is, would we put to practice what we know to do in doing our part to produce the kind of home that hard work takes? And discipline? Part of that discipline is to be kind and submissive to our husbands. This, too, is against nature.

The man has to learn to lead, and we are the helpers even in that. He is going to make many wrong decisions, and we are going to have to discipline ourselves with God's help to forgive him. Just as we have to learn to be a wife and mother and learn to love, he has to learn to lead and to be a good husband and father.

⁓ He Trusts in Her

"The heart of her husband trusts in her, and he will have no lack of gain. She does him good and not evil all the days of her life" (Prov. 31:11–12).

It takes time for him to trust in her. It takes time to be trustworthy. Our husbands have to know that we are on their side all of the time. We need to be their best friend. We want this home to live and prosper and to be a monument to God. We need to tell our husbands over and over these things. And that does not mean we uphold his error or sin.

⁓ He Trusted Her Financially

Statistics say that most divorces happen now because of finances. A wealthy man was asked to what he contributed his success in finance. He said, "1 wanted to see how much money I would need to make before my wife could spend it all."

But the worthy woman "considers a field and buys it; from her own earnings she plants a vineyard." (How many husbands today would allow a woman to buy land?)

This woman could be trusted to be wise. Wise in her selection of land, wise in her need of land, and wise in using her own money to plant the land.

On the other hand, young couples want to start out with what the older couples have attained through a lifetime. They do not realize the different stages of financial lows and highs that have been experienced in their parents' lives. The bride today wants sterling silver and crystal. Her mother or grandmother rejoiced when the ten-dollar rent could be paid.

God wants us to have a comfortable living and our pleasant houses. But He wants us to have them in time. We short circuit His plans when we strive for things to the disregard of home and happiness. He will richly supply our needs in His good time. Over and over, He tells us what He wants us to have. He tells us that He can give so much better gifts than we can give to our own children. But He knows in His wisdom that we will not appreciate what we have if we have it too soon.

Once when I wrote a check for my groceries, a young lady asked me incredulously, "Do you have the checkbook? My husband would never let me have the checkbook." We had to learn to share it. Hopefully they will learn too.

Surely the lack of leadership, submission, and knowledge of God's Word will lead to an unhappy and unfulfilled life. Older women are charged with the responsibility to help out the young women. Patience is hard for young people, and yet the best way is the way of waiting on the Lord and growing together, trusting and trustworthy.

WILLING TO ADAPT

"Willing to adapt themselves to their husbands" was what one of the versions used for the term "subjection." The ideal way is for the husband to lead and the wife to adapt. Daily. With most decisions, he should lead, and she should follow. This means time together to discuss and to talk things over. Quality time as well as quantity. It is a means of progress. Shall we rent or buy? Trade cars now? Where can we afford to go for a vacation? Shall we buy new shoes for one of the children this payday, or can the shoes make it until the next one? Each day has its problems and decisions to be made. We advance by making a good decision together. We even learn through the wrong decisions—the painful ones.

Communication is the key! It is always the key. "Following after the things that make for peace" is another factor. Treating our husband the way we would like to be treated is a giant plus. How important it is to have sympathy for his position of having to make the decisions and forgiving him for the wrong choices is another.

∼ TENDERHEARTED

Now we can see God's direction when He puts kindness before submission. Kindness leads to submission, not vice versa. When I get crossways with my husband and am super critical, I have to step back and work on kindness. Then it all falls in place again.

I work at remembering that we are all children—sheep—and terminal. None of us knows how to go in and go out. If I were leading, I wouldn't know the answers. It would be the blind leading the blind. The man usually thinks more wisely than the woman does. More horse sense.

God tells Titus, "Let the older woman talk this way to the younger. They will take it better from her than from you." Women can agree together that we are not long on a lot of the right answers. Our emotions get in the way. Why does the door-to-door salesman prefer talking to us? Because we'll buy!

"Be gentle and do as their husbands tell them." If you were a man, wouldn't you dread "going to the mat" for every decision? Wouldn't you appreciate it if she could be easily won to your way of thinking?

He put within womankind the desire for peace. We are unhappy when our husbands are unhappy or displeased with us. This desire for peace is a gift from God to both of us—the husband and the wife.

THE EXCEPTION

Though we are to follow their lead, we are not to go across God's commands. God is always to come first. "We must obey God rather than men" (Acts 5:29).

If Sapphira had not agreed with Ananias in lying about their giving, she would have saved her own soul and life and maybe his. But they agreed together to sin (Acts 5). If Abigail had abided by Nabal's decision to ignore David and his army (1 Sam. 25), she would have been a party to a massacre of innocent men. But she did what was right. Our moral strength can be an unbelievable encouragement to our husbands. We cannot compromise on sin. We cannot agree together to sin nor can we blindly follow error.

God told women in 1 Peter 3:6, "Just as Sarah obeyed Abraham calling him lord, and you have become her children if you do what is right without being frightened." Do what is right and do not be fearful of the consequences.

SUMMARY

God never commands something that He won't help us do. We are blessed if we have had in our own raising the example of a gentle loving woman who helped to keep peace and order in the home.

But God's forethought provides for those of us who did not have that precious example. We too can learn how to cooperate and become the helper that we want to be. Older women should be our examples and teachers.

Young women should bear in mind that they too will be called on for teaching younger women someday. We have all heard that old saying that "as goes the home, so goes the nation." Something is wrong when well over half of the nation has divorced.

Part of the cause is the lack of solid homes that have produced children who have lost their way. Husbands must lead and wives must follow for the happiness of the home and the pleasing of God.

"Love is not measured by how many times you touch each other, but by how many times you reach each other"—Anonymous.

Be good to yourself. Love your husband and adapt to him.

Love, Lea

⟫⟫⟫ PAUSE AND PONDER ⟪⟪⟪

In what ways do you have a problem being submissive? What can you do?

A Happy Home

It has been God's plan from the very beginning for man to be the head of his home. Wise is the woman who submits to his authority and blessed is the man who understands her willing submission. Happy is the home where Dad rules lovingly and is himself submissive to Christ.

> *Being in subjection to their own husbands.* This is fully in keeping with the New Testament teaching that the husband is the head of the family; and, through the centuries, those societies in which women have honored this divine injunction have invariably elevated women to higher and higher places of honor, respect, and protection. In many cultures where this ethic is dishonored, women have ultimately been reduced to the status of chattels, as they were in the pagan culture of Paul's day. The behavior here enjoined proved to be the way up for womankind; and the opposite of it will doubtless prove to be the way down.[51]

God has put great emphasis on husbands here in Titus 2. In fact, all seven qualities we have described have something to do with a husband. As we have mentioned beforehand, the list begins with a man and ends with a man. Our man. And just what will we do with it, ladies?

A WOMAN'S PRAYER

Our Father, we thank You for making us women. We thank You most of all for making us Your daughters. We praise You and bless Your glorious name. Please help us to be obedient to Your will and not our own. We are so blessed to have a husband, dear Lord. And we ask You to bless him with a good life, and may we please You, our Father, by being submissive to him as we are submissive to You. We love You with all our being. Thank You for giving us this life. In Jesus' name. Amen.

THOUGHT QUESTIONS

1. Is submission really necessary to the Christian home? Why?
2. How can a wife prove to her husband that she can be trusted with the checkbook?
3. Name some results that occur when the wife willingly adapts to her husband.
4. What happens when a wife won't submit to her husband?

♪ **Song:** "It Is Well with My Soul"

Insights

A Spiritual Awakening

The Father has created us to be social human beings. We especially need Him, and we need each other. Let's reflect on all who have already crossed our paths. We need friendships and relationships to help us daily. Who can walk the narrow paths, the valleys, and the "remnant" roads without God and the friends He sends our way? As I write this, it is the year 2020, a year that will go down in infamy. I have learned from COVID-19 that the social distancing, the extreme separating of ourselves from others, the huge dots and x's on the floors to direct us, and all the lockdown of families and religion have resulted in one thing: loneliness. Sheer loneliness. Anyone with me on this?

Why was I lonely? I missed my spiritual family, the local congregation—my spiritual brothers and sisters. I missed the three-times-a-week gatherings and ladies' Bible classes on Tuesdays. I missed our touching, our hugs, and all the encouraging words. I missed our fellowships—the eating side by side. I missed the laughter of the kids—my kids, my family, the church. I just wanted to sit and see everyone's face again! Our congregation livestreamed its services and continues to do so. What a plus that is for those who have compromised illnesses and cannot leave their homes! But I have to admit there is a huge temptation for the Christian to neglect the services resumed at the church building in favor of the convenience of gathering around the laptop.

There is nothing that compares to being together, side by side and face to face. Our congregation closed its doors for approximately four weeks. When we all were finally able to worship again and sing together, I think we all cried! The Hebrews 10:25 passage was written to encourage first-century Christians not to forsake the assembly, and it still means the very same thing for the twenty-first-century Christian: "Not forsaking our own assembling together, as is the habit of some, but encouraging one another; and all the more as you see the day drawing near."

When a human being hears and obeys the gospel call of Jesus, then the Father places that individual in His family—God's family. Let's look for a moment at the new life of that very first congregation of the Lord's body in Jerusalem.

> They were continually devoting themselves to the apostles' teaching and to fellowship, to the breaking of bread and to prayer. Everyone kept feeling a sense of awe; and many wonders and signs were taking place through the apostles. And all those who had believed were together and had all things in common; and they began selling their property and possessions and were sharing them with all, as anyone might have need. Day by day continuing with one mind in the temple, and breaking bread from house to house, they were taking their meals together with gladness and sincerity of heart, praising God and having favor with all the people. And the Lord was adding to their number day by day those who were being saved. (Acts 2:42–47).

The six verses above are full of action and love, aren't they? Do you sense any loneliness at all? To me, it is all "togetherness." The church is the family of God where we worship, live for God, and love one another. This is our home. This is where we belong. This gathering of people will produce many BFFs in our lives. But we must always remember that this family is not perfect. We are not perfect. We all make mistakes. Only Jesus was perfect. And just as we must ask forgiveness from God for our sins, we must also ask for forgiveness from the sisters and brothers of our spiritual family. Keeping the slate clean with any friend is crucial if we want that relationship to last and endure.

I once saw a huge billboard that said: *WANT TO BE LOVED? BE LOVABLE!* True, right? Be loving. Be friendly. Be open to people. Yes, it makes each of us vulnerable, but love is worth it. How did Jesus act with people? Was He unfriendly, rude, distant, harsh, or uncaring? Absolutely not. In fact, the picture that the four gospel writers paint for us is a Savior like no other: open, affectionate, compassionate, loving unconditionally, truly interested in any soul that crossed His path—and absolutely fearless when it came to setting any error or person straight. People were comfortable with Jesus.

> *Who took advantage of these opportunities to learn more about God?*

Who would think that out of something strange and deadly, a blessing can arrive? A new birth can occur? It can, and you have been a part of it and probably didn't even know it.

If I remind us of 2020, I think I will hear a collective groan. So what were we concerned about that year? Where was our focus? What were we reading? Where were our minds? How were we living Philippians 4:8? We were in the middle of the pandemic. No sports; no movies; few restaurants were open; most churches closed; schools closed. However, Romans 8:28 teaches us that God causes all things to work together for good for His children. Perhaps God was using this time for a spiritual renewal in our hearts and in our congregations. Excellent sermons streamed from the internet by committed Christian preachers. It was easy to livestream, and the potential for spiritual growth remained. The question that must be asked is, who took advantage of these opportunities to learn more about God and grow in the faith?

On the other hand, there was a definite temptation to never leave home again for worship. Why get up, get dressed, and make the trip to the church building when one really didn't need to darken the door of the building ever again? Worship became a "pajama event" with breakfast and coffee in bed while the laptop aired the preacher's sermon. Somehow I don't think that is what the psalmist meant when he wrote in Psalm 29:2, "Ascribe to the Lord the glory due to His name; worship the

> *Was God testing our love, our faith, and our commitment to Him?*

Lord in holy array." Perhaps there were even those who worshiped via livestreaming any day they chose. Sunday was no longer the Lord's day, and that certainly freed up the weekend! Who would know? God would. And that's not what God prescribed for us.

When the pandemic hit, my Jeff and I were most happy to be able to worship online with our brethren. We also liked the flexibility of watching other preachers online. But I have to admit that something was missing. What was it? That missing link was that I was not present with the church physically.

Not hugging and seeing fellow Christians made me feel like a bounced check, null and void. I missed the singing the most. I have heard others say the singing is what they missed the most too. This time away from my brethren has made me value our Sundays and Wednesday evenings together now. Worshiping together is more special, more heart-warming, more meaningful. Maybe God was trying to wake us up again. God knows how stubborn we humans can be, how obstinate in our habits and thinking. So perhaps God wanted us to see one another from a different perspective.

Was COVID-19 a test from God? Did we test positive or negative? Was God testing our love, our faith, and our commitment to Him? A Christian must look at this pandemic and ask, "What did God want me to do? What was He trying to teach all of us?" And we know from Hebrews 10:25 that the possibility of forsaking the assembly plays into this. It seems that church attendance was a problem even in that first-century church.

> Let's hold firmly to the confession of our hope without wavering, for He who promised is faithful; and let's consider how to stimulate one another to love and good deeds, not forsaking our own assembling together, as is the habit of some, but encouraging one another; and all the more as you see the day drawing near (Heb. 10:23–25).

Yes, these are strange and difficult times, but that is nothing new. Hopefully, these times are only temporary, as life surely is. It is difficult to quarantine ourselves. The real question is, "How much do I love God and His family?" Brothers and sisters need to be together, laboring for the Master. And when we are absent from one another, we are just an arm or a leg, out there all alone, longing for family members who make up the rest of the body.

> For the body is not one member, but many. If the foot says, "Because I am not a hand, I am not a part of the body," it is not for this reason any the less a part of the body. And if the ear says,

"Because I am not an eye, I am not a part of the body," it is not for this reason any the less a part of the body. If the whole body were an eye, where would the hearing be? If the whole were hearing, where would the sense of smell be? But now God has placed the members, each one of them, in the body, just as He desired. If they were all one member, where would the body be? But now there are many members, but one body (1 Cor. 12:14–20).

In essence, we all need one another in order to function properly. When you and I became Christians, the Lord put us into His family. And this is where we belong, being obedient to our elders, on the Lord's day. We are simply not whole and complete unless we are all together.

Perhaps our Father is looking down from heaven and seeing who really loves Him and truly lives for Him. What happened when things returned to normal? Did some never darken the door of the church building again? Yes. Some had to be encouraged to return to live worship. All we can do is encourage. At the end of the day, sweet sisters, you and I have to take care of our own souls and put ourselves to the test by asking, "How much do I really love the Lord? Enough to worship with fellow Christians and not lazily in my recliner?"

> *We need one another in order to function properly.*

This reminds me of Psalm 53:2, "God has looked down from heaven upon the sons of men to see if there is anyone who understands, who seeks after God." God knows everything. He is omniscient. We don't fool Him at all. When He looks down from heaven now and gazes at His family, does He see anyone who understands and seeks Him?

Yesterday was Sunday, the Lord's day, and at our congregation, we assembled to worship in the morning and in the evening. After the morning worship, I was walking from the auditorium into the foyer, noticing the groups of Christians, my family, who were deep in conversations or running after their children. Everything was right again and friendly and good—even with masks on—a warm spirit everywhere I looked. I thought to myself, "Oh, Beck, what was that scripture about being in the Lord's house is better than——?" Here it is:

For a day in Your courts is better than a thousand outside. I would rather stand at the threshold of the house of my God Than dwell in the tents of wickedness (Ps. 84:10).

Being in the Lord's house, being with the brethren, is the most fulfilling and thrilling thing I will ever know. This is home. I needed to be reminded of that again. So pause for a moment, my sister, and reflect. What did the Father teach you that impresses you the most about the pandemic and your relationship with Him? Fill in the blank and tell me your answer someday. I would love to know.

The Father has taught me that _____.

CHAPTER 10

Never, Never MOCK God's Precious WORD

"that the word of God may not be dishonored"

*W*hat is the final result of an older woman training a younger woman to have the seven godly qualities of Titus 2? What do you think God's goal is here? Let's pause and look at this Titus passage one more time.

> Older women likewise are to be reverent in their behavior, not malicious gossips nor enslaved to much wine, teaching what is good, so that they may encourage the young women to love their husbands, to love their children, to be sensible, pure, workers at home, kind, being subject to their own husbands, so that the word of God will not be dishonored (Tit. 2:3–5).

Girls, we often overlook that last phrase. Hear what it says: "So that the word of God will not be dishonored." Dishonored here is the Greek word *blasphemeo*, which has the meaning to speak reproachfully, rail at, revile. *Blaspheme* means "to curse, to swear." One dictionary says: "to speak impiously or irreverently of; to speak evil of, to slander, abuse."

Here are some parallels for the phrase, "that the word of God may not be dishonored" (Tit. 2:5 NASB).

- ❖ That the word of God be not blasphemed (KJV)
- ❖ A good advertisement for the Christian faith (J. B. PHILLIPS)
- ❖ That the word of God may not be discredited (RSV)

Somehow we miss this part of the passage. Most of us get stuck on Titus 2; many of us want to argue with God about Titus 2, but few of us see God's purpose in giving us Titus 2. It is the bottom line of why God wants older women to help the younger women. This is God's goal in all things, dear sisters. Don't miss it!

How Dishonor Behaves

God tells Paul to tell Titus to tell the older women what kind of women they ought to be in order to encourage the younger women to be what they ought to be. Why? Here is the zinger: We women have to be all these things so that people do not make fun of or mock or curse God's Word!

Can't you just hear the world say things like this:

- ❖ "And you go to what church?"
- ❖ "Well, if that's what a Christian family is like, I want no part of Christ!"
- ❖ "And you call yourself a Christian?"
- ❖ "Is that what your Bible teaches?"

Titus was instructed by Paul to tell the church in Crete what type of Christians they were to be. The Cretan citizens had their eyes focused on the behavior of the church members. John Dummelow, in his commentary in the early 1900s, wrote: "The Cretans would say, 'See how they treat their husbands, that is Christianity!' " Sure makes me think of that old saying by William Toms, "Be careful how you live. You may be the only Bible some person ever reads."

What Do We Reflect?

Wouldn't it also be fair to say that we women are to love one another and mentor one another so that we do not bring reproach on our Father? We are the image that the world sees when it looks at a Christian woman. We are the image the world sees as it looks at a Christian family. Our supreme desire is to reflect God and our obedience to His precious Word, the Bible, hoping others will obey His Word too. If the world sees conflict and rivalry between sisters in the church, we have brought dishonor upon the very words of God. Why would anyone be drawn to Jesus or even want to become a Christian if they see us mistreating the very ones we are supposed to love?

God won't have it, girls! We must open the Bible, look at Titus 2 honestly, and obey it with all our hearts. Why? So that God's precious Bible will be respected and not mocked. So that the Bible will be held in reverence and not laughed at. So that all people—Christians and non-Christians—will realize that this most treasured gift from the mouth of God has been given to all men and women. Why, why, why? God wants us to know Him. And the only way we are ever going to know God is to read God. All of this is serious, serious stuff. All of this is serious, serious business. Who would really want to cause the world to make fun of God?

Learn from Jackie's Story

I once worked with a woman who brought great reproach upon the church. I had known her years before, as we had worshiped together before our family moved to another congregation. I had not seen "Jackie" for at least twenty years. On my first day of work at this company, Jackie and I recognized each other and hugged.

We chatted a few minutes and returned to our duties. A coworker then asked, "Do you know Jackie?" I said, "Yes, we went to church together a long time ago." "You went to church together?" she asked me. "Yes, we did," I answered. My coworker then replied, "Well, Jackie has one of the worst mouths I have ever heard in my life." With those words, she turned and walked away. Unfortunately, I found her words to be true.

As I meditate on Titus 2, Jackie's story keeps popping into my mind. You see, Jackie is the sad example of a sister who never got the training God wanted her to have. But there are two sides here. The first side is that possibly Jackie never had anyone in her life who cared about her enough to train her, help her, guide her, and exhibit what a Christian woman should look like. The other side of this story could be that women had tried to help her, and she rejected their efforts.

Actually, there is a third side to all of this, and this one is the most frightening. Could it be that Jackie really didn't want to grow as a Christian should? Could it be that God, His love, His Son, and His commandments meant nothing to her? Could it be that Jackie was a Christian in name only? Could it be that Jackie wanted to live her life "her way," so she bucked God's authority?

Whatever the reason, Jackie's behavior, her foul mouth, and her lifestyle all made Titus 2:5 come true.

You see, Jackie hurt God. She dishonored Him. She brought reproach on Jesus who had gone to the cross and died for her. Her ways hurt God to such an extent that through her language and lifestyle, Jackie continuously brought reproach on His church and His marvelous book, the Bible. How tragic! None of my coworkers wanted to attend the church of Christ. I hope I changed that kind of thinking.

My sisters, always remember: The world is watching us. The workplace gossips about Christians, mocks Christians, and ridicules Christians. But the workplace secretly respects those who live and act like Jesus. Our mission is to win souls for God, not win souls for Satan.

⇢⟩⟩⟩ PAUSE AND PONDER ⟨⟨⟨⟵

Perhaps you know someone like Jackie. Have you ever been embarrassed by another Christian's behavior? What can you learn from that experience? What scripture encourages you to honor Him with your life?

Ignorance Is Bliss!

My precious sisters, Titus 2 is one of the most crucial passages in the entire Bible to be heeded and obeyed. And do you know what I have discovered? Christians don't look at this passage—they just keep on turning to something else in the Book. The thinking is: "If I don't look at it, I can pretend it isn't there, and then, I don't have to do it!" Now, how stupid can we be?

My dad once studied with a woman who represented that attitude. She didn't like what the Bible said about a controversial topic. So she told my dad, "That's not in my Bible!" She opened her Bible, turned to the chapter, and she was right; it wasn't there. She had cut it out!

Not only has the Lord shown us what He wants from older men, older women, young women, and young men, but He expects His children to meld them into their very beings. If the Lord said it, He expects us to do it. That old saying, "The Lord said it; I believe it; that settles it" is actually wrong. It should be: "The Lord said it and that settles it." The Lord rules, girls. Period.

Adding Things Up

David once wrote in Psalm 119:160: "The sum of Your word is truth, and every one of Your righteous ordinances is everlasting." What does *sum* mean? Well, to most of us it means the total of adding items up. And when you take God's Word from Genesis through Revelation, what you have all totaled is the Truth of God. Remember Jesus saying to His Father in John 17:17: "Sanctify them in the truth; Your word is truth"?

When an older godly woman encourages a younger woman to love her husband, love her children, be sensible, be pure, be workers at home, be kind, and be subject to her own husband, that which is totaled up is the truth—the true woman of God. Here she is pure and unadulterated—God's woman.

Barclay summed it up this way.

> There is no greater task, responsibility, and privilege in this world than to make a home. It may well be that when women are involved in the hundred and one wearing duties which children and a home bring with them, they may say: "If only I could be done with all this, so that I could live a truly religious life." There is in fact nowhere where a truly religious life can better be lived than within the home.
>
> In the last analysis there can be no greater career than that of homemaking. Many a man who has set his mark upon the world has been enabled to do so simply because someone at home loved him and tended him.[52]

MOM SAYS

So God's Work Will Not Be Blasphemed

There are only a few words left—one more teaching still untaught. It is a very potent, disturbing phrase given in closing.

It proves these teachings are not just casual advice but warnings for the soul, as are all of God's teachings.

Are these words said as a plea from God to His daughters, or are they a straight look in the eye from the Father? Or both? We see examples of God in both circumstances under the old law.

We see Him plead and beg Israel to come back to Him, to return to righteousness. "Why will you die, O Israel? For I have no pleasure in the death of anyone who dies," declares the Lord God. "Therefore, repent and live" (Ezek. 18:31–32).

We also hear Him say, "As I swore in My wrath, they shall not enter My rest" (Heb. 4:3). And He let them wander in the wilderness for forty years, children of God, until they died. Only two righteous men of the original travelers made it to Canaan.

Maybe the words are so rightly written that they can move the love of the tenderhearted or get the attention of the stubborn. He knows how to do that. The first are moved by His love and the latter by His power.

Many times as we read the past ten chapters, especially for the young women, Satan tried to jar the reception. He is a static causer. He tempts us at our weakest points. Remember how many years' experience he has had!

But, thank God, God is greater and much more powerful than Satan. "Because greater is He who is in you than he who is in the world" (1 John 4:4).

Satan's greatest tool is deceit. He fools us. He lies to us and we believe him! He is the father of every lie. He is after our souls.

Will we allow ourselves to believe that through our stubbornness or naivete we can be guilty of causing God Himself to be dishonored? Do we believe that is even possible? Satan says it isn't.

Does the Father get that involved in our lives? Does He care if my husband is unloved or my children neglected? Does it really concern Him if I am not a home-lover? Does He note my indiscretions, unkindnesses, or lack of hospitality? Do I insult Him when I insult my husband? (That hurt!) Does He care when I tear down my own house with my own hands and sit and cry in the rubble?

But a much more important question is the one God is asking us: Do you care when your actions hurt Me? Each of us will have to answer that question individually.

God pronounces a woe to those who have evil and good all mixed up in their thinking:

> Woe to those who call evil good, and good evil; who substitute darkness for light and light for darkness; who substitute bitter for sweet, and sweet for bitter! Woe to those who are wise in their own eyes, and clever in their own sight! (Isa. 5:20–21).

It is hard for women today to believe that the world is wrong and God is right. We can't help being influenced by the conduct of others! Some answer thus; "How can we live with being the only woman in the block that stays home and is 'just' a housewife? This teaching is two thousand years old! I don't have the courage or inclination to swallow it." Yet His words echo in our hearts, "I know the plans I have for you . . . plans for welfare and not for calamity to give you a future and a hope" (Jer. 29:11).

The real problem is getting our want-tos straight. This is a hard decision. But where does it say that being a Christian is easy? A cross is never easy to carry or drag. But God tells us that the reward at the end of the way is worth it all! I believe that. Don't you?

Pray about it. God's ears are open to His daughters. How quickly He hears our petitions. Do you remember when good King Hezekiah was told to get his house in order, for he was going to die? Isaiah the prophet had brought this bad news. Hezekiah wept and reminded God of his own good life and service. He begged to live. He cried. Note how quickly his prayer was granted.

> Before Isaiah had gone out of the middle court, the word of the Lord came to him saying, "Return and say to Hezekiah the leader of My people, 'Thus says the Lord, the God of your father David, I have heard your prayer, I have seen your tears; behold I will heal you. On the third day you shall go up to the house of the Lord. I will add fifteen years to your life'" (2 Kings 20:4–6).

> It will also come to pass that before they call, I will answer; and while they are still speaking, I will hear (Isa. 65:24).

That is how anxious He is to help us. But we often have not because we ask not. God hears the prayers of the righteous, but He turns away His ears when we won't listen to Him.

"For the eyes of the Lord are upon the righteous, and His ears attend to their prayer, but the face of the Lord is against those who do evil" (1 Pet. 3:12). What does God call evil? Disobedience of

His Word. "He who turns his ear from listening to the law, even his prayer is an abomination" (Prov. 28:9).

It is a two-way street, and because we care for Him, we will listen and revise our life. Come to think of it, isn't that what we are supposed to do daily? We must remember it is His love for us that causes Him to give out the warnings and instructions. Will we take Him at His word, or will we endanger His good name? The choice is ever ours. That's fair, isn't it? God's plans for our welfare are always conditional. Be ever conscious of the "ifs" or the "whens."

In Jeremiah 29, He tells of His marvelous plans and then He gives the conditions.

> Then you will call upon Me and come and pray to Me, and I will listen to you. You will seek Me and find Me when you search for Me with all your heart (Jer. 29:12–13).

That's work and probably a lot of suffering too.

"LORD, ARE YOU SERIOUS?"

Lord, do I really have to do everything You say?
Don't I get to do some things my very own way?
Isn't Your book just full of suggested things to do?
Hints full of wisdom, proposals, often true?
Or are Your words still wonderful words of life?
Could they really have the power to quench my pride
    and strife?
Surely in all this time they've lost some of their power,
Can no longer give the strength to each waking hour.
But a solemn thought from Him keeps probing as it
    ever comes my way.
"The words I've said will judge you when we meet on
    Judgment Day!"

—Lea Fowler

THOUGHT QUESTIONS

1. Why is deceit such a powerful weapon for Satan?
2. Are God's words commandments or just good advice? Explain.
3. What does the word *blasphemy* mean?
4. What does disobedience to God's Word mean for the Christian?

A WOMAN'S PRAYER

Our Father, please, please forgive us of our sins. Please let us come into Your presence and bow at Your feet. We know we don't do things right, and we know that we make many mistakes. Please help us to see the right things to do in this Christian life, and Lord, help us to do them. When we do these right things, we are obeying You. And when we obey You, we are truly happy. Help us to keep our eyes on You. We love You so. Please, please forgive us. In Jesus' name, Amen.

♪ **SONG:** "Trust and Obey"

Insights

Look at These Marriages

Perhaps you have read the following two articles before. They are excellent commentaries on wedded Christian bliss or wedded Christian nightmare. This I do know; they should be read by every teenager and every Christian contemplating marriage.

I found "I did not marry a Christian" on Facebook. My friend who placed it there does not know who the author is, but the message is worth your reading.

I Married a Christian

I married a Christian because a godly wife is a blessing to any man. The genuine spirituality of a companion is worth far more than rubies or all the treasures of the earth. Truth, mercy, and loving-kindness are her garments for every day. I married a Christian because of the hours of trial on the path of life. Her wise and understanding heart is a strength in moments of discouragements and despair. She is longsuffering toward human weaknesses and knows that victory comes from a bond of genuine Christian love. When the hour is dark and all seems hopeless, she shows me the silver lining in the cloud of trouble. I married a Christian because I know my love will be returned a hundred-fold. I know that I have that which I give and her love too. Our aims, our hopes, and our aspirations are one. This brings true happiness in our companionship.

I married a Christian because I wanted a companion with a Christ-like mind and attitude to counsel the family. My children are blessed with a clean comfortable home and a mother who will listen to their problems of life with a loving heart. I married a Christian because her love looks beyond her own family to the sicknesses and needs of others. She seeks first God's kingdom and His righteousness. She sets the proper example for our children. I married a Christian because I can love, trust, honor and cherish her until death parts us. I married a Christian because I want more than anything to go to heaven when this life is over, and I believe she does too. We can help each other as we journey the road of life; that we may both live in heaven after a while.[53]

I Did Not Marry a Christian

I read the article titled "I Married a Christian" with great interest and it drove home some very sobering thoughts. As I read the article, I could not help but think of what a contrast my own life was, for you see, I didn't marry a Christian.

No one told me of the unhappiness I was due in marrying a non-Christian. At the time I married, my parents were not faithful, and consequently neither was I. I can't put the responsibility for my actions on them; I was eighteen and knew what the Bible taught on marriage.

Now after having lived with a non-Christian for almost ten years, I have been made aware of how important it is for our young people to marry Christians. These ten years have not made me an expert on the subject, but they have made me realize that I should try to teach and/or discourage others from making the same mistake.

When I fell in love with my husband, I could not think about those things that could lay ahead. The only thing I knew was that I loved him with all my heart and no one knew or had experienced this kind of love. Ours was different as I felt there was nothing that could ever come between us that we could not overcome.

I was soon to realize how our attitudes and thinking varied. We rented a small apartment and were soon entertaining non-Christians in our home. The drinking and dancing were all part of the things I had been taught to abhor. And yet, right here in my own home I was consenting to, and becoming a part of, things that a Christian has no business doing. I was getting further and further away from the church. I knew what I should be doing as a Christian, and yet I was doing nothing to change. We were happy by most people's standards, but I was miserable. I knew my husband did not share my love for the truth, and he was not serious-minded about things like that. I loved him so much, but I was learning a hard, cold fact—love was not enough. I wanted to return to my "first love." We talked about my return to the church, and I realized another fact—he had no intention of going with me in spite of his promises (before marriage) that he would.

I decided to wait about returning and try to work things out as best I could. In the meantime, we found out we were expecting our first child. I was elated! I also was made aware of the creation of God within me. I was soon to become a mother and have a life truly influenced by me. I was going to get my heart right with God again.

I repented of my sins and started trying to live the life I so wanted to live. It was hard. First, because I had no encouragement from my husband, and second, because we still had all our non-Christian friends. My Christian friends came by, but not too often because my husband openly did not like them. I loved them and wanted them in my home. I needed them. Somewhere about this time, the hostility began. I was seeing and hearing a different guy from that wonderful guy I married. There was a wall building between us. Out of love for my husband, I again stopped attending church. I did not attend for months. I was miserable inside again. After the birth of our daughter, I wanted to get started back to church. My husband's answer was no. He wanted me to start going to church with him where he went as a child—a denominational church that did not follow God's Word. We really had problems there. I knew the error they taught, and I could not worship there. He insisted; I resisted.

Three-and-a-half years ago I repented again and started to live the Christian life. I thank God that He spared my life and let me live long enough to get back. There is no turning back for me. We have three children now, and I want more than anything to have a Christian home for them. This presents another problem. My husband and I do not agree on how to bring up the children. We are both pulling in different directions. I believe in teaching them to put God first and to be faithful. He still can see no reason to attend every service and openly overrides me when I insist the children go.

Our marriage has deteriorated greatly over the last few years. The "church problem," as my husband put it, has moved into every aspect of our marriage. We both keep things bottled up inside and find that we can't talk things out anymore. I am ill with the children much too often. I know it's because things are not right between my husband and me.

My marriage has reached a disastrous point. My husband has given an ultimatum. I have to make a choice—him or the church. Those of you who are Christians know what a rough decision I had. I, of course, have chosen the Lord. I still love my husband with all my heart and have prayed that God would open his heart to understand the truth. I know I have to remain faithful and do what God has commanded me to do. It looks so dark sometimes, and yet I must "press on toward the goal for the prize of the upward call of God in Christ Jesus" (Phil. 3:14). I'm so weary from being torn between my husband and the Lord.

To our young people, I'll say that God frowns on mixed marriages. In 2 Corinthians 6:14–15, we are taught not to become unequally yoked together. The damage done is not just to yourself, but to your husband or wife and then to your children. My prayer is that this article may in some way encourage our young people, or anyone planning to marry, to marry a Christian. I can't do mine over again, but I can teach my children and others how important it is to marry a Christian and to make that home the kind the Lord intended for it to be.[54]

Marital Advice from My Mother
by Martha Coletta

My mother was a city girl. My father was a country boy. They met and dated very briefly during World War II. It was a time of quick romances and impulsive marriages. Their life together lasted twenty-three years, producing four daughters. I am the eldest, now in my seventies.

On my wedding day mother and I had a quiet moment together before driving to the church building. She shared a piece of advice which I have always treasured. She said, "Learn to support your husband in whatever it is that he wants to do. Encourage him in major decisions he is trying to make, and let him know that you will always be there for him."

My parents were so different from each other. Mom, the city girl; Dad, the country boy. They made it through World War II, the Korean War, and part of Viet Nam. But their wants and priorities were so different; they pulled in opposite directions and were not happy. Sadly, they separated right before my marriage. I have always thought it curious, if not tragically poetic, for Mom to give me that advice as I was about to place my hand in Frank's.

We were married five years when Frank and I put on Christ in baptism. A year later the Northeast School of Biblical Studies started where we worshiped to prepare men to preach the gospel. Frank's desire was to be in that first class. It meant leaving his teaching position at the local high school. It meant stepping out on faith and trusting that God would supply our needs. We had two little girls and a monthly mortgage payment. I was a stay-at-home mother. How I have always given thanks for Mother's counsel to stand with my husband and say, "I support you in this decision, Frank. We will be okay."

Our extended families thought we were nuts. "You're quitting your job? Your retirement? Your health insurance? How are you going to pay your bills? This is crazy!" Others laughed and taunted, "What are you going to eat? Your Bibles?"

God did provide for us. We never missed a bill payment; we gave faithfully to the work of the church. While we didn't always eat steak, we never missed a meal and our growing girls wore perfectly fine hand-me-downs. We often refer to those two years as Our Camelot Years, a time of complete immersion into the study of God's Word. We never regretted our decision to take that step of faith.

I continue to hold to Mother's advice, even though she didn't realize its influence. Perhaps she'd be pleased to know that it has been passed on to our daughters also.[55]

CHAPTER 11

The Power of BEAUTIFUL Lives

A phrase in *Halley's Bible Handbook* encapsulates Paul's instructions for all categories of Christians. The Titus 2 passage is titled, "The Power of Beautiful Lives."

> Aged men, aged women, young women, mothers, young men, and slaves are exhorted to be so faithful to the natural obligations of their own station in life that critics of their religion would be silenced.[56]

I truly believe that God wants positive, secure, and happy children who will do His work with those same attitudes. It is an honor to be God's child! Why should any of us be sad? It is an honor to have heard the gospel of Jesus Christ, to have been washed in His blood, and to have set upon the path that leads home. I think of David's song of trust: "The lines have fallen to me in pleasant places; indeed, my heritage is beautiful to me" (Ps. 16:6).

The life our Father has given us—the "lines," the boundaries that surround us daily—are pleasant and beautiful, no matter where we are. Learning to surrender ourselves to His will becomes our goal. Heaven awaits us, and nothing is more important, as the old song says, "The Way of the Cross Leads Home."

What Do You Do When—?

What do you do when you are a younger woman, desiring the friendship, encouragement, help, and teaching from an older woman, and no one steps up to the plate? What do you do when the older women in the congregation simply are not connected to the younger women and refuse to be?

Perhaps the congregation is very small; perhaps the congregation is made up of ninety percent senior citizens; perhaps you are on the mission field, and you have only your family to help you. The "what ifs" can go on and on. That is exactly where Leslie found herself.

Leslie's Story

"Becky, your topic [about mentoring] is so important. As a young mother in my early twenties, I longed for a godly woman to mentor me, not only in raising godly children and being a godly wife, but more than anything I needed and longed to be mentored by a godly woman of faith/belief and trust in God. I subconsciously searched for an older woman of faith, only to be disappointed. Jesus didn't entrust Himself to any man because He knew what was in the heart of man (see John 2:24–25). In 1 Peter 2:23, Jesus kept entrusting Himself to God who judges righteously. Neither should we entrust ourselves to man but to God. It was then that I decided and realized God could be my teacher and guide. It was one of the most important lessons for me. I am learning to be that woman of faith I needed so desperately back in my twenties. God, I believe, purposely lead me in that direction so I would learn from Him. I am not negating the importance of mentorship. I believe it is a vital part of what it is to be part of the body of Christ. We all need to be mentors. We all need to encourage others and help them. Since I became open to what teaches me about faith, it has been my heart's desire to teach others about faith and trust in God. But even beyond mentoring, we need to show them Jesus: 'fixing our eyes on Jesus, the author and perfecter of our faith' (Heb. 12:2). And we need to demonstrate that He is the Teacher and the Guide in our faith and in all things."

> Ask, and it will be given to you; seek and you will find; knock, and it will be opened to you. For everyone who asks receives, and he who seeks finds, and to him who knocks it will be opened (Matt. 7:7–8).

Ask, Study, Serve, Trust

Could Leslie's story be ours? Yes. But let's go a step further and ask, What do we do when we need more spiritual teaching and guidance, and the church has no one to help? I ask this because there have been times that I needed more biblical knowledge and deeper teaching, and no teacher was available.

❖ *First, we must pray.* Pray and give it to God. Pray and toss it to Him. Tell Him what is on your heart. Yes, He already knows. Let Him work on it. Don't fret and worry. Remember, it's all in God's hands anyway. Several hundred years ago, Martin Luther said, "Pray and let God worry!" Isn't that a great way to put it? But instead, what happens to us women? We have to drag the problem around in our mind, rehearse it over and over, fret, fret, fret and worry, worry, worry. Learning to cast our worries on the Lord is hard for many sisters, but what do you think God wants? God wants to be in on every aspect of our lives; He inspired Peter to write, "Casting all your anxiety on Him, because He cares for you" (1 Pet. 5:7).

I live in the huge state of Texas, and hundreds of small towns with small churches of the Lord's body dot the map. As I drive through these small towns, I am often struck with the thought, "What kind of teachers and preachers are here? Are the Christians knowledgeable and well versed? What do these small churches do when they want to grow in the faith and there is little knowledge to be shared or few capable teachers?" They should ask God for help. Tell Him of their spiritual needs. Then what?

✧ *Second, do something about the problem.* As the saying goes, put "feet on your prayers." They can ask themselves, "What does God want us to do about this problem?" Each person can ask, "What can I do?" And every time the answer is the same: Get in the Word and study! Then get to work.

No matter what problem you or the church is having—and trust me, every church has problems—put on your shoes and equip your heart to serve the Lord. Visit the members. Take food to the shut-ins. Give yourself away. Don't dwell on what the church doesn't have, but dwell on what it does have. Believe it or not, things could be worse!

Nothing is impossible with God, so watch how easily He will fill the needs of your congregation. He may send a worthy and loving teacher—just what everyone needed! Or God may send some families with young children, so you will experience a growth spurt. Trust God to heal the problem.

✧ *Third, realize that God is the best teacher.* Trust Him to teach you. Leslie mentioned this when she said, "It was then that I decided and realized God could be my teacher and guide . . . It was one of the most important lessons for me . . . God was my teacher and guide in all things."

Leslie, that is the answer to every problem we will ever have! Our Father knows how to help; He has the answers! Trust Him, do His work, and He will send the blessings.

A Woman of Faith

My precious sisters, let's take responsibility for our own Christian growth. We decide how spiritual we are going to be. We decide how much we will give to our marriage and to our children. We decide how sensible and submissive we will be. We decide whether to be kind and pure. We decide how committed we will be to this thing called Christianity.

Are we women of faith? Are we in The Book? These words may have been written two thousand years ago, but they still are essential in every aspect of our Christian walk with God today. "So faith comes from hearing, and hearing by the word of Christ" (Rom. 10:17). Not only must we be women of The Book, but also obedient women.

My sisters, I think we forget how much the Father loves us. He wants us to be happy, secure, and positive Christians, living good lives for Him. Satan wants us miserable, insecure, and negative, living meaningless lives for him. Whom will we choose? In *The Help*, Constantine, played by Cicely Tyson in the movie, observes, "Every day you're not dead in the ground, you wake up in the morning, you gonna have to make some decisions."

What will we do with God's directives in Titus 2? Will we claim them and obediently work them into our daily living from this moment on? Or will we read them and disregard them for the rest of our lives?

I do know that there is no second guessing God. What God has said, He means. How imperative that we take the Father seriously. The problems in the Cretan church had to be addressed so the church could grow properly. And then God inspired Paul to instruct Titus on how to correct those problems. When He gave the answers, did He expect to be obeyed? Of course.

Surely we are all aware that the world watches Christians and the church and observes our behavior, speech, and manner of living. No matter what we do or say, we reflect the Father. What Christian wants to bring reproach or criticism upon God? Rather, don't we desire to hear the community around us say, "These Christians really practice what they preach"? Don't we sing, "They'll Know We Are Christians by Our Love," with all our might?

Thank You, Older Women

Whether we like it or not, God's words are in the Bible, in black and white, and have been there hundreds of years, calling His creation to examine, heed, and obey. I know what it is like to be a younger woman with a very busy husband, children, and a life that desperately needs another woman's help. My heart is so full of thanks to those older women who loved me enough to train and encourage me spiritually. Thank you for getting out of your comfort zone and courageously obeying God's command to teach me in loving my husband, loving my children, being sensible, being a worker at home, being kind, and being submissive to my husband. Thank you for helping me not to mock God's Word or cause others to mock God's Word because of me. I am most blessed, for I know that in my own life, God has sent just the right teachers, mentors, sisters, and brothers when I needed them the most.

Listen to these thoughts on encouragement:

> The church is so badly in need of men and women who make it their ministry to encourage others by exerting a positive influence, opening doors of opportunity, and helping fellow Christians triumph over disappointments and mistakes. You can nip discouragement in the bud by helping those around you to bloom. Make it your business to do all you can to assist others in fulfilling their spiritual potential.[57]

> The older women must teach and train the younger. There are those who use their experience to discourage others . . . It is a Christian duty ever to use experience to guide and to encourage, and not to . . . discourage.[58]

What If They Won't Listen?

The older woman has the heavy task of training the younger woman to be God's woman. First, she must take her role seriously. The older woman has to be not only approachable, but she must also be godly and loving before she can help the younger woman attain what God has prescribed for her. Like the old saying goes, "You can lead a horse to water, but you cannot make him drink." An older woman can pray all the prayers; she can teach all the lessons; she can live out the Christian life every possible moment for the young women to see. But it is up to the younger Christian woman to choose to obey God.

> In case the older women should not have been successful in inculcating these noble virtues in the younger women, as Paul admonished, the apostle was sure that the word of God would "be blasphemed." So much depends on the women, in great part on the young women. *The world still judges Christianity by the character of the young women produced by the church.*[59] (emphasis mine)

MOM SAYS

THE ANSWER BOOK

When I was a child, we occasionally had books in school that included the answers to questions asked or problems to be solved. These answers were in the back of the book.

God gives us a detailed answer book. He entreats us, begs us to look to Him for a happy and abundant life. He wants us to have wisdom, to know how to direct our daily lives, to have a good marriage, faithful children, a loving husband, peace of mind, and finally how to get home to Him.

Often we want a quick answer with little study. We even want to copy another's paper. We want to pass the test and have all the blessings with as little involvement as possible. And that's impossible. We want to look in the back of the book.

We don't want to eat it or it to eat us. We gain a little "head knowledge" but not a lot of "heart knowledge." As I heard someone say, "We want to live like the rich man and die like Lazarus."

THE GIVER

God is love, and God is the greatest of givers. He stands and knocks at the door of our hearts asking to come in and sup with us. He even provides the feast, literally and figuratively. But He never force feeds. Rather, His plea is, "Come, now and let us reason together" (Isa. 1:18). The next verse says, "If you consent and obey, you will eat of the best of the land." Consent to what? Obey what? Sitting and reasoning with God.

One of the saddest verses in all the Bible is Ezekiel 33:11. "Turn back, turn back from your evil ways! Why then will you die, O house of Israel?"

The church is the house of Israel now. We have our answer book in our hands. What can be done to help us love it, study it, and meditate upon it? Who can persuade us to take the gift of God into our hearts?

SUMMARY

God, through Titus, instructs the older women to help the younger women. Hopefully the younger women will welcome the reasoning together of the two. Hopefully the younger will reach for the out-stretched hand of the older.

He gives us a list of things to talk about and to work on. Then He closes the list with the thought that these things must be taught and practiced. If they are not practiced but are disregarded, then God's Word would be blasphemed. If we learn to really love His Word, we will not only be free from blasphemy, but we will also sail our ships to a safe harbor.

When all is said and done, we still have to ask ourselves: How much do I really want to please God? Am I pleasing Him now with the way my home is? Am I ready for every good work? Are my children and husband happy? Is Christ proud of me? Do I love the Word of God and do I share it with others?

I close with this admonition:

Pay close attention to yourself and to your teachings; persevere in these things; for as you do this you will ensure salvation both for yourself and for those who hear you" (1 Tim. 4:16).

You will help to save your house. That's all Noah saved.

Love,
Lea

Our Cloud of Witnesses to Servanthood

The story of Job is mesmerizing. Job was a man who lost all he owned: his children, his servants, and his herds. Then he suffered painful, bodily sores. God called him "My servant." Job had done no wrong, and yet he suffered. But he never stopped loving God.

Was there a mightier king than David, the shepherd king of Israel? Do you know of any king whose heart was more of a servant's heart than his? His desire was to do the will of the Lord and to obey Him in all things, not to mention the way he loved God's law. Even though David made mistakes and committed the tragic sins of adultery, murder, and deceit, God still loved David. And don't forget that God forgave David. Did David have to pay the consequences of his sins? Oh yes. And yet, it is only about David that God says, "I have found David the son of Jesse, a man after My heart, who will do all My will" (Acts 13:22).

And what about a woman named Phoebe? Paul was impressed with her servant's heart and praised her with these words:

> I commend to you our sister Phoebe, who is a servant of the church which is at Cenchrea; that you receive her in the Lord in a manner worthy of the saints, and that you help her in whatever matter she may have need of you; for she herself has also been a helper of many, and of myself as well (Rom. 16:1–2).

She was a worker; she was a doer; she was a helper, not in the arena of Greek society, but in the Lord's work. That was number one with sister Phoebe. Can't you just picture her, working from house to house, providing food and shelter for Paul and for others, serving, and more serving? She didn't just help Paul and his ministry, but she was "a helper of many." I picture Phoebe as a real live wire! Imagine being praised by God through the apostle Paul!

When I read these accounts of Job, David, and Phoebe, I see three people who loved, obeyed, and served God no matter their circumstances. And they were surrounded by difficult times. I am struck by my own inadequacies. I can do more. Can't we all? Of course. Let's remember our passion for the Lord and why we became a Christian in the first place. Let's remember that old rugged cross and the sacrifice Jesus made for us there. Let's remember Titus 2 and what the Lord wants from all of us. Does God ask too much of us? Never.

Oh that the Lord would say the very same words about us that He says about Job, David, and Phoebe.

PAUSE AND PONDER

Write your name in the following blanks.

"Have you considered My servant _____?"

"I have found _____, a woman after My heart, who will do all My will."

"I commend to you our sister _____, who is a servant of the church, that you receive her in the Lord in a manner worthy of the saints, and that you help her in whatever matter she may have need of you; for she herself has also been a helper of many."

What Is My Mission?

Paul's words come to my mind as we close. "For to me, to live is Christ and to die is gain" (Phil. 1:21). "For if I preach the gospel, I have nothing to boast of, for I am under compulsion; for woe is me if I do not preach the gospel" (1 Cor. 9:16).

Our mission on earth is to spread the gospel of Jesus, and Paul surely felt its urgency. Christians are the vessels that carry that gospel to a lost and dying world, and do we feel the same urgency? Ask yourself: "Am I obedient to whatever God asks of me?" If not, then how in the world can I possibly teach others to open up the Bible, to love God and to obey God? The world will never be drawn to rebellious children of the Lord. They will only be drawn by children of God who look and act like Jesus.

Sometimes we see spiritual things from only one side. We have tunnel vision. We read Titus 2 and see the list of qualities God wants us to obtain, and we stop right there. We might think, "Sister So and So sure needs to read this!" Seldom do we read God's Word further and find the answers as to why God requires these behaviors. Titus 2 hits all of us women. Never forget the last part of verse 5, "that the word of God may not be dishonored."

The Plan

Our merciful and compassionate Father looks down from heaven and sees our priorities and where we place Him. Don't forget that He has a plan for us. How exciting to know that the Creator of the universe knows our names and has a mission for us. Note again His words to His children of Israel which also apply to His children today:

> "For I know the plans that I have for you," declares the LORD, "plans for welfare and not for calamity to give you a future and a hope. Then you will call upon Me and come and pray to Me, and I will listen to you. You will seek Me and find Me when you search for Me with all your heart" (Jer. 29:11–13).

I saw a quote by Ben Heber on Facebook that said, "The greatest waste in the world is what we are and what we could have become." As a Christian woman, I want to rephrase that to say, "The greatest tragedy in the world is what we truly are and what we could have become for God." We can argue; we can complain; we can throw up our hands and walk away if we want. We certainly can refuse to do anything God says. God will let us do whatever we desire. He gives us that choice. But His Word is true, and He still said it. And, like it or not, God wins every time. His way is the only way, and trust me, He always has the last say. Don't we want to please Him?

The Woman I Want to Be

Recently I read this saying: "Noah didn't know what an ark was. Noah didn't know what rain was. But he knew who God was."

Do we know who God is? Are we daily in His mighty Word? We don't have to comprehend every word that God speaks. We know who He is, and that is all we need to know. We must be women of faith who know God and walk with Him. To love God is to obey God.

Nothing is more important than our love for God; He is our passion and our life—here and in the world to come. What will you do, my sister? What will I do? Let's take to heart the words from the old preacher who said, "God is just sitting on ready, ready to change your life!" Nothing is impossible with our God, and He will help us change and become what we need to become.

God calls to us in 1 Corinthians 15:58: "Therefore . . . be steadfast, immovable, always abounding in the work of the Lord, knowing that your toil is not *in* vain in the Lord."

Will we be stubborn women who refuse to change or bend? Or will we be the Lord's servant? Even Job, the man who was "blameless, upright, fearing God, and turning away from evil" had to repent (Job 1:1; 42:6). We all must do whatever it takes to get our lives right with God. Heaven is too important to miss! My precious sisters, it doesn't matter what I say. It doesn't matter what you say. The only thing that matters on this planet is what God says.

A WOMAN'S PRAYER

My precious Father, I love You so much, and I praise Your glorious name. I want to live for You and not for myself. Father, may I never, ever mock Your holy Word or cause others to mock or dishonor the Bible. Please, Lord, don't give up on me. I want to walk with You and please You and do Your will for me, and not my own will. Help me to work Your plans for me. Help me to be like Jesus, so selfless and obedient. I give You my all, Lord. Please don't ever stop loving me. I will always be Your daughter. In Jesus' name. Amen.

THOUGHT QUESTIONS

1. How do we get closer to the Word?
2. What can cut between the soul and spirit of man?
3. How can we save our homes?
4. What does it take to change ourselves?

♪ Song: "Blest Be the Tie"

Insights

A Sentimental Journey

This book has been a very emotional journey for me, traveling again with my mom down a road that she carved and blazed. When my son Jeffrey and I were discussing this book once, he said, "Mom, this book is like that song, 'Unforgettable.' You know, Natalie Cole and her dad Nat King Cole, singing it together. That is you and your mom."

Yes, that is right. Mom and I are singing together. Thank you, precious, precious Mother, for loving me and teaching me to love God and to surrender to His will. Thank you for writing *Precious Are God's Plans* and especially for showing me the way home. I miss you so much.

I have felt Mom's presence all during this book's writing. I have felt her humor and yet more than that, her insistence that this book "get done!" In skimming over the manuscript one day, my eyes fell on her words,

> When will we ever learn that when God speaks, it is not just for instruction, but it also is to tell us that this is the only way that things work? He just says, "Do it this way." It takes us a long time to learn that this is the only way.

May we always remember that it's all about God and what He has written and not about us and how we think things should be. We do not always have it right. Our Father tells us so. Proverbs 14:12 says,

"There is a way which seems right to a man, but its end is the way of death." Jeremiah 10:23 says, "I know, O Lord, that a man's way is not in himself, nor is it in a man who walks to direct his steps."

Recently, a quote by Elisabeth Elliot found on Facebook really hit the nail on the head: "We can't really tell how crooked our thinking is until we line it up with the straight edge of Scripture."

Jesus' prayer in Gethsemane comes to mind continually: "Father, if You are willing, remove this cup from Me; yet not My will, but Yours be done" (Luke 22:42). Our prayer should be, "O Lord, please give us a loving and obedient heart to do Your will and not our own. We want to be obedient from the heart like Jesus."

Paul's letter to the church at Philippi stands out as a favorite of many Christians as it is a letter of encouragement. Philippians 4:9 in particular is quoted repeatedly by Christians. Common English Bible's modern translation reads, "Practice these things: whatever you learned, received, heard, or saw in us. The God of peace will be with you."

Surely this passage falls heavily on any conscientious brother or sister whose greatest desire is to please the Father. Paul boldly urged the Philippian church to practice right thinking and Christian service, to live in the same manner as their leaders.

Does verse 9 strike your heart at all? Does it prompt you to ask yourself if you could write these same words to other Christians? Could you ask your brethren to imitate your life because you were living spiritually correct? Paul wasn't bragging; he knew that he was walking with the Lord, pleasing the Lord, living completely as he should for the Lord. Paul also knew that he was a forgiven sinner. There was no doubt in Paul's mind that he was living each day as righteously as he possibly could. His conscience was clear.

Are we to that point, my sister? I don't know about you, but I have much work to do on ol' Beck before I can implore anyone to live like I live. God is not through with me, and I fall on my face daily before His merciful throne to thank Him for loving me and being so patient. The following words were mentioned several chapters ago, but let's look at them one more time:

> Women of God can never be like women of the
>   world.
> The world has enough women who are tough; we
>   need more women who are tender.
> There are enough women who are coarse; we
>   need women who are kind. There are enough
>   women who are rude; we need women who are
>   refined.
> There are enough women of fame and fortune; we
>   need women of faith.
> We have enough greed; we need more goodness.
> We have enough vanity; we need more virtue.
> We have enough popularity; we need more
>   purity.[60]

Mom was not like women of the world. She lived the above quote with such passion. She continues to inspire me, challenge me, and set a fabulous example of the Worthy Woman. Lea Fowler would go anywhere, anyplace, anytime to teach anyone the gospel of Jesus. I know the Father loved her and blessed her richly, and I also know I need to be more like her. God isn't through with me yet, and I honor Him most of all, continually giving thanks for His mercy.

Thank you for traveling with Mom and me on this sentimental journey. The Christian life is the trip of a lifetime with heaven in mind. Come and walk with us, my sisters.

May each one of us prayerfully approach His throne (Heb. 4:16), lay our burdens down and say, "Oh, Lord, thank You for loving me. Please forgive me, and please give me the strength and knowledge to change. Please help me to work Your plan, my Father. More than anything Lord, I want to be Your Precious Woman!"

Always remember, Mom and I will meet you at The Gate. The best is yet to come.

I sure do love you. Love, Becky

WHEN THE LAST CHILD LEAVES

The last one cleaned his bedroom out; he left
    today at five.
There was not much to talk about; his car backed
    down the drive.

This is the first night they all slept behind some
    other door.
This is the first night these rooms keep our
    children safe no more.

They were our own to hold; we had them for that
    time
When they could not yet handle cold and needed
    help to climb.

You loved them, Lord, before the day they came
    into our sight.
You love them more than words can say—Please
    love them well tonight.

—Robert Stanley

Endnotes

1 Mary Farrar, *Choices: For Women Who Long to Discover Life's Best* (Sisters, OR: Multnomah Books, 1994), 153.

2 Lea Fowler, *Precious in the Sight of God* (Fort Worth, TX: Quality Publications, 1983), 8, 10.

3 Burton Coffman, *Coffman Commentaries on the Bible*, Titus, https://www.studylight.org/commentaries/eng/bcc/titus.html.

4 William Barclay, *The Daily Study Bible*, 2nd edition, *The Letters to Timothy, Titus, and Philemon* (Philadelphia, PA: The Westminster Press, 1960), ix.

5 David Lipscomb, edited with additional notes by J. W. Shepherd, *A Commentary on the New Testament Epistles*, Vol. V, *Commentary on I, II Thessalonians, I, II, Timothy, Titus, and Philemon* (Nashville, TN: Gospel Advocate Co., 1942), 267–268.

6 David Lipscomb, edited with additional notes by J. W. Shepherd, *A Commentary on the New Testament Epistles*, Vol. V, *Commentary on I, II Thessalonians, I, II, Timothy, Titus, and Philemon* (Nashville, TN: Gospel Advocate Co., 1942), 272.

7 Burton Coffman, *Coffman Commentaries on the Bible*, Titus 2:4, studylight.org/commentaries/eng/bcc/titus-2.html, accessed April 30, 2021.

8 Carl Spain, *The Living Word Commentary*, Vol. 14, *The Letters of Paul to Timothy and Titus* (Abilene, TX: Abilene Christian University Press, 1984), 178.

9 Lon Woodrum, https://scripturalteachings.wordpress.com/2012/01/31/service-to-god-and-man/.

10 Jerome K. Jerome, https://www.goodreads.com/quotes/574752-it-is-in-our-faults-and-failings-not-in-our.

11 Burton Coffman, *Coffman Commentaries on the Bible*. Titus 2:4–5, studylight.org/commentaries/eng/bcc/titus-2.html, accessed April 30, 2021.

12 Adam Clarke Commentary, Titus 2:3, https://www.studylight.org/commentaries/eng/acc/titus-2.html.

13 https://www.brainyquote.com/quotes/marianne_williamson_635483.

14 M. Scott Peck, *The Road Less Traveled: A New Psychology of Love, Traditional Values and Spiritual Growth* (New York, NY: Simon & Schuster, 1978), 84–85.

15 J. J. Turner, Ph.D., *7 Ways to Wreck a Marriage* (Huntsville, AL: Publishing Designs, Inc., 2014), 7, 9.

16 Betty S. Bender, *What's a Woman to Do?* (Nashville, TN: 21st Century Christian, 1993), 51–52.

17 Burton Coffman, *Coffman Commentaries on the Bible*, Malachi 2:16, accessed May 3, 2021, https://www.studylight.org/commentaries/eng/bcc/malachi-2 .html.

18 J. J. Turner, Ph.D., *7 Ways to Wreck a Marriage* (Huntsville, AL: Publishing Designs, Inc., 2014), 98–99.

19 Patsy Loden, *Loving Your Husband* (Huntsville, AL: Publishing Designs, Inc., 2014), 197.

20 Don McWhorter, *God's Woman: Feminine or Feminist?* (Huntsville, AL: Publishing Designs, Inc., 1992), 59–60.

21 Betty Bender, et. al., *Mentor Me* (Huntsville, AL: Publishing Designs, Inc., 2020), 129.

22 Ruth Hulbert Hamilton, "Song for a Fifth Child," *Ladies Home Journal,* 1958. http://www.lullaby-link.com/song-for-a-fifth-child.html.

23 Worldometer, "Abortions This Year," accessed Aug. 19, 2021, https://www .worldometers.info/abortions.

24 Burton Coffman, *Coffman Commentaries on the Bible*, Titus 2:4, studylight. org/commentaries/eng/bcc/titus-2html, accessed May 19, 2021.

25 Robert W. Firestone, Ph.D., "Eight Reasons Parents Fail to Love Their Kids," *PsychologyToday.com*, Oct. 7, 2015, accessed May 19, 2021. https://www .psychologytoday.com/us/blog/the-human-experience/201510/8-reasons -parents-fail-love-their-kids.

26 Dave Roos, "Latchkey Kids: What's Different about Leaving Children Home Alone Now Versus Then," HowStuffWorks.com. Statistics from 1982. Accessed Aug. 19, 2021, https://health.howstuffworks.com /pregnancy-and-parenting/latchkey-kids-children-home-alone-now-then .htm.

27 "The Lonely Life of Latch-Key Children, Say Two Experts, Is a National Disgrace," *People* magazine, 1982.

28 Burton Coffman, *Coffman Commentaries on the Bible*, Matthew 5:22, StudyLight .org. https://www.studylight.org/commentaries/eng/bcc/matthew-5.html.

29 Wayne Jackson, *A New Testament Commentary* (Jackson, TN: Christian Courier Publications, 2012), 476.

30 Burton Coffman, *Coffman Commentaries on the Bible*, Titus 2:4, studylight. org/commentaries/eng/bcc/titus-2.html, accessed May 19, 2021.

31 Merrill F. Unger, *Unger's Bible Dictionary* (Chicago, IL: Moody Press, 1966), 1205.

32 Heartsill Wilson, "The Beginning of a New Day," Pinterest.com.

33 Washington Gladden, "In the Bitter Waves of Woe," *The Treasury of American Sacred Song with Notes*, No. 217, https://hymnary.org/text/in_the _bitter_waves_of_woe.

34 Wayne Jackson, *A New Testament Commentary* (Jackson, TN: Christian Courier Publications, 2012), 476.

35 Martha Peace, *Being a Titus 2 Woman* (Bemidji, MN: Focus Publishing, Inc., 1997), 100.

36 Frank Chesser, *Thinking Right About God* (Huntsville, AL: Publishing Designs, Inc., 2014), 188–189.

37 Lea Fowler, *Precious Are God's Plans* (Fort Worth, TX: Quality Publications, 1986).

38 Lea Fowler, *Precious Are God's Plans* (Fort Worth, TX: Quality Publications, 1986).

39 *Henry Ward Beecher,* https://www.sermoncentral.com/sermon-illustrations /52822/we-are-always-in-the-forge-or-on-the-anvil-by-by-sermon-central.

40 *Albert Barnes' Notes on the Whole Bible*, Titus 2:5, accessed June 2, 2021. https://www.studylight.org/commentaries/eng/bnb/titus-2.html.

41 *Matthew Henry's Complete Commentary on the Bible*, 1 Timothy 5:13–14, accessed June 2, 2021, https://www.studylight.org/commentaries/eng/mhm /1-timothy-5.html.

42 *Adam Clarke Commentary*, Titus 2:5, accessed June 2, 2021, https://www .studylight.org/commentaries/eng/acc/titus-2.html.

43 Wayne Jackson, *A New Testament Commentary,* 2nd Edition, (Stockton, CA: Christian Courier Publications, 2012), 476.

44 Betty Bender, *What's a Woman to Do?* (Nashville, TN: 21st Century Christian, 1993), 90–92.

45 David Lipscomb, *A Commentary on the New Testament Epistles,* Vol. V. *I, II Thessalonians, I, II Timothy, Titus and Philemon* (Nashville, TN: Gospel Advocate Company, 1942), 273.

46 William Barclay, *The New Daily Study Bible,* 2nd Edition, *The Letters to Timothy, Titus, and Philemon*, Titus 2:3–5, (Philadelphia, PA: The Westminster Press, 1960), 286–287.

47 Author Unknown, "The Temper Poem," MargiesMessages.com, accessed June 7, 2021, https://www.margiesmessages.com/angertemper.html.

48 Isaac Watts, "The Almost Christian," Hymnary.org, accessed June 7, 2021. https://hymnary.org/text/broad_is_the_road_that_leads_to_death

49 Author Unknown, *Family Times*, "Dreamed of Death Coming," accessed June 7, 2021, https://www.family-times.net/illustration/Judgment/202768.

50 Betty S. Bender, *What's a Woman to Do?* (Nashville, TN: 21st Century Christian, 1993), 126–127.

51 Burton Coffman, *Coffman Commentaries on the Bible*, Titus 2:5, accessed June 8, 2021. https://www.studylight.org/commentaries/eng/bcc/titus-2.html.

52 William Barclay, *The Daily Study Bible Series*, Revised Edition, Titus 2:3–5, accessed June 11, 2021, https://www.dannychesnut.com/Bible/Barclay/TimothyTitusPhilemon.htm.

53 Anonymous, via "K. E. Family Lifeline," September 2, 2001.

54 Posted on Facebook by Dave Hart. Source unknown.

55 Martha Coletta. Source unknown.

56 Henry H. Halley, *Halley's Bible Handbook* (Grand Rapids, MI: Zondervan, 1965), 643.

57 Aubrey Johnson, *The Barnabas Factor* (Nashville, TN: Gospel Advocate Co., 2005), 129.

58 William Barclay, *The Daily Study Bible,* 2nd edition, *The Letters to Timothy, Titus, and Philemon*, Titus 2:3-5, (Philadelphia, PA: The Westminster Press, 1960), 285.

59 Burton Coffman, *Coffman Commentaries on the Bible*, Titus 2:22, accessed June 18, 2021. https://www.studylight.org/commentaries/eng/bcc/titus-2.html.

60 Margaret D. Nadauld, "The Joy of Womanhood," accessed July 19, 2021. https://www.azquotes.com/author/52736-Margaret_D_Nadauld.

CPSIA information can be obtained
at www.ICGtesting.com
Printed in the USA
JSHW031127150222
22934JS00002B/2

9 781945 127236